THE FAILURE
ADVANTAGE

THE FAILURE
ADVANTAGE

Why Setbacks Are Your
Secret Weapon for Success

MATTHEW EGAN

Copyright © 2025 by Matthew Egan

All rights reserved. No part of this book may
be reproduced or used in any manner without
written permission of the copyright owner except
for the use of quotations in a book review.

FIRST EDITION

978-1-80541-786-6 (paperback)
978-1-80541-785-9 (ebook)

About The Author

Matthew Egan is a business transformation and operations specialist with over 20 years of experience leading change at organisations, including Microsoft and PwC. Throughout his career managing teams, working with C-suite executives, and driving transformation projects, he has observed how setbacks can either limit potential or serve as powerful catalysts for growth.

Matthew is a Fellow of the Institute of Chartered Accountants, and recipient of multiple business accolades, but it's his personal experience with anxiety and failure that shapes his approach. Having faced his own professional challenges, he's passionate about helping others transform their relationship with failure.

Originally from Australia and now based in the UK, Matthew lives with his wife and son, who continue to teach him the most valuable lessons about embracing imperfection and finding opportunity in adversity.

www.matthewegan.net

CONTENTS

About The Author v
Introduction 1

Part 1 : Break free from fear

1. The hidden cost of playing it safe 15
2. Choose a better story 33

Part II : Turn setbacks into stepping stones

3. Failure is just feedback 59
4. Focus on what you can control 81

Part III : Progress over perfection

5. Start before you're ready 105
6. The power of small wins 123

Part IV : Balance safety and challenge

7. The courage to be vulnerable 143
8. Embrace productive discomfort 169

Bringing it all together 189
Further resources 195

Introduction

They say you should write the book you need to read. So here it is. I've realised my fear of failure has held me back, causes me anxiety, and could prevent me from reaching my full potential. I've also realised that many others suffer from this problem. The symptoms vary, from not acting on your biggest dreams to beating yourself up when things don't go your way, but the root cause is the same: seeing failure as an end point rather than a necessary stop on a journey. It is likely reducing your ambition and sucking the enjoyment from life. But here's the good news: by digging into my own failures and mindset patterns, I've discovered something amazing. We can completely rewire our relationship with failure. Even better, those painful setbacks we've been avoiding? They might actually be our greatest competitive advantage.

Let me share what I've learnt.

One of my many failures

I remember the moment clearly. Actually, I'd been building to that moment for years, and the words seemed to echo louder than they should have. I was sitting across from the managing partner of my firm, who would deliver the news I'd been waiting for—whether or not I'd be admitted to the partnership. He came straight out with it: "You'll have to wait another year," he said.

But in that moment, it didn't feel like postponement; it felt like a door slamming shut. For someone like me, who had spent more than a decade methodically climbing the corporate ladder—ticking every box, doing every assignment, and being told repeatedly that I was on the right path—this wasn't just a career setback. It questioned everything I knew about myself.

Looking back now, I can see that this moment, and the decisions I made and its aftermath, was pivotal. It revealed the limits of my understanding of failure. At that moment, though, all I could see was the end of a dream. I left the firm shortly afterward, and for years, that failure stayed with me.

But the failure started years earlier. I started my journey at the firm while I was still at university, and it was the only career I had ever known or aspired to. Becoming a partner wasn't just a goal; it was *the* goal. I didn't have familiarity with other workplaces, other careers, or other occupations. My field of vision was so narrow that all I had seen was those who went before me, treading a very similar path. The only logical thing to do, really, was to follow.

Over the course of a decade, I followed the path others had taken before me. I excelled in my roles, hit every milestone, and received constant affirmation that I was partner material. I took on challenging assignments, moved overseas for a period, worked in unfamiliar business lines, and consistently proved my ability to adapt and deliver.

By the time I was 31, I was ready for my assessment for partnership admission. This involved putting together a sound business case, understanding the business line where I could make money, building a good network of contacts with potential clients, and importantly, being well-networked within the firm. These were boxes I had dutifully ticked with the support of mentors in the final few years.

So, when the rejection came, it was unlike anything I'd ever faced up to that point. My career had been defined by success; failure—true painful failure—was a foreign concept. The shock of not being accepted wasn't just professional; it was personal. It attacked my identity. I saw myself as a partner, or at least as partner potential, and for the first time, I felt like I wasn't good enough.

In the days and weeks that followed, I cycled through every stage of grief. I blamed others—the firm, the market conditions, the politics of the partnership process. I blamed myself, questioning whether I'd been truly good enough. And I blamed the world in general, falling into a spiral of resentment and bitterness. Ultimately, I saw the rejection not as a delay but as a definitive end. I closed the door on the firm and began looking elsewhere.

What I now know is that my bruised ego drove me to prove that I could be successful outside the firm. Within months, I'd moved on to a new role. But here's the thing: while I've achieved success in other ways, I never became the partner I once dreamt of being. And now, looking back with clearer perspective, I see how flawed my response to that failure was.

I focused on the superficial reasons for my rejection—timing, relationships, external factors. I never truly reflected on what I could learn from the experience or grow from it. My reaction was to give up, not to adapt. Looking back, I think now: "If I'd been truly passionate about it, I could have easily done another year." It was an annual process of partner admission, and effectively, that year I could have learnt from what I'd failed on previously and potentially strengthened my case to make for a better partner.

Now, just for the record, the way things have turned out in my life have been overall incredibly positive, so I don't know if this alternative path would have been any better or led to any better outcomes than what I've achieved now. But I do know that I gave up at that point. It wasn't a conscious choice; it was just a habit because my identity had been attacked.

What if my approach to failure had been different? What if, instead of retreating, I had leant into the discomfort and asked myself: "What can I learn from this?" I believe the outcome would have been entirely different.

What I know now is that my approach to that failure, and many others since, was deeply flawed. Not only did I needlessly give up on a long-held aspiration, nor did I take the benefit of the learnings available and apply them to become better. Some 13 years have passed since and it is only recently that I have realised this attitude toward failure has been standing in the way of my own growth, development, and life enjoyment. And I see others in the same situation every day. In this book I want to share what I have learnt about failure and show how changing your relationship with it can turbo charge your own growth and help you get more out of work and life.

We're conditioned to avoid failure

But why did I respond the way I did and why has it taken me so long to realise it? The problem I believe is that failure, particularly in big business, is taboo. From an early age, we're conditioned to fear it, avoid it, and, when it eventually happens, to hide it. In business, this mindset manifests in a relentless focus on success metrics, a cultural aversion to risk, and a tendency to bury our mistakes rather than confront them.

This likely stems from a few sources. First, most businesses are built on selling things, and selling things requires marketing and sales. Marketing and sales focus on accentuating positives and benefits, often at the cost of hiding detriments. Big business thrives on projecting an image of competent success and forward momentum. Marketing campaigns and sales pitches highlight wins, growth, and competitive edges. The word *failure* is scrubbed out because it doesn't align with the polished corporate narrative. But this is a distorted reality, where risks, missteps, and failed experiments are hidden. Teams feel pressured to downplay setbacks and present incomplete truths, leading to poor decisions, marketing spin, and skewed product narratives. Consider a product launch that fell short of expectations. Instead of analysing and sharing the failure internally, it gets reframed as a partial success—missing critical lessons in the process.

Another dynamic is management incentives. Management compensation structures in big business often prioritise outcomes—revenue growth, profit margin, and stock performance—over processes or experimentation. On one level, this alignment of stakeholder and management interests makes sense. However, the system penalises risk-taking. Short-term incentives encourage short-term thinking, leaving no space for experimentation or developing better long-term outcomes. Managers, in turn, become risk averse. Teams learn to "game the system", setting conservative goals to ensure success—even if it means underperforming their potential.

Next is the social comparison problem. This isn't restricted to big business; it shows up in our personal lives as well. In recent years, this issue has been accentuated by the growth of social media. Companies, and the people within them, don't exist in a vacuum. People compare themselves, both professionally and personally, driving an obsession with looking good rather than being honest.

We only need to spend 10 seconds looking at our phones to see how success and failure are regarded. Social media feeds are jammed with people leading their "best life". We're led to believe the average person is up at 4:00 a.m., working on their six-pack, meditating, teaching the homeless, jetting off for high-powered meetings, rescuing a kitten, *and* earning a doctorate. All before breakfast. Where are the examples of people sleeping past their alarm, striking traffic on the way to work, getting nothing done, wasting money, or failing to complete their to-do lists? All these things are erased for fear someone might find out.

That's just at the individual level. In workplaces, this problem becomes ingrained in the culture. Employees compare their performance and progress to peers. The great human resource "innovation" of the last 30 years, the bell curve, has amplified this. Annual performance cycles stack-rank people to determine rewards and career progression, further ingraining this social comparison. The result? People are trained to look around and compare themselves to others.

Finally, there's a career stigma around failure. A person's career can be defined by either succeeding or failing, and because careers make up so much of our identities, people become too attached to the outcome. This means they focus on presenting a particular image rather than working on the process itself. More time and energy are spent on *looking* successful rather than putting in effort.

So, it's no wonder you avoid failure at all costs.

Failure comes before success

But avoiding failure also avoids success, because failure doesn't need to be an end point, but rather progress that moves you forward.

Given the impossibility to remember everything, our memories tend to record ultimate outcomes and achievements rather than the journey. The same is true of how we record history. Captain Cook is known for discovering and charting the coast of Australia as opposed to the experience he gained serving in the Seven Years War or mapping the St Lawrence River in Quebec. George Washington is known as a founding father and America's first president as opposed to a skilled mathematician and land surveyor. This tendency to distil a series of activities and events into single outcomes also results in us glossing over the many failures that are the precursors to success. We forget that failure and success are not mutually exclusive, nor statements in perpetuity.

Penetrate the veneer of some of our most revered identities and you'll find events that, at a point in time, would have been complete failures. One notable example is Abraham Lincoln. Today, we see him as the president who held the country together during the Civil War and wrote the Emancipation Proclamation. His Gettysburg Address is still talked about today. But if you looked at his life in the mid-1850s, you'd see a different story. His first business venture as a store owner in New Salem, Illinois, ended badly, leaving him in debt for years. He lost his first bid for the Illinois legislature in 1832. When he finally entered politics, he was defeated for Speaker of the Illinois House in 1838, and he lost his nomination for Congress in 1843. What's really striking about Lincoln is that he kept facing setbacks. After one term in Congress, he became so unpopular for opposing the Mexican American War that people thought his political career was over. He then lost two Senate races in a row, especially the notable one in 1858 against Stephen Douglas, where voters rejected him even after he gave great speeches during their debates. Before he became president, Lincoln had actually lost more elections than he had won.

Or then there is Harland Sanders, known to the world as Colonel Sanders or the founder of KFC. Many people don't realise that the Colonel was 62 when he found a restaurant owner in Utah who agreed to sell his "Kentucky Fried Chicken" recipe. Or take J. K. Rowling, rejected by multiple publishers before turning *Harry Potter* into a global phenomenon.

Modern business and societal pressures urge us to push away failure. But look at any remarkable success and I guarantee that most will have come following, and perhaps as a result of, many earlier failures.

Don't let past failure limit your future potential

If you're reading this book, then I'm guessing you may be an anxious achiever. Someone who, by many measures, is successful but still feels something is missing or carries around a burden of doubt or uncertainty despite external success. Perhaps you've already climbed the corporate ladder to the top and are thinking: "Is this it?" Or perhaps you're starting at the bottom and are fixated on the next promotion or career milestone, eagerly comparing yourself to others on the same journey. Or perhaps you have great external success but constantly berate yourself on what could have gone better or where you "should" be by now. I can relate to all of these and see many others in the same position every day.

The typical response from achievers is to simply work harder. To do more hours, produce more, work earlier, work later, squeeze more in. This may work for a period, which validates the approach. But sooner or later it comes tumbling down. You hit a bump in the road that brings into question everything you have been doing. Every failure presents an obstacle between where you are and where you want to be—something that needs to be overcome or pushed aside as quickly as possible to move forward. Then the next obstacle comes, and the next, and the next and after a while you are so exhausted that you give up, question your ability, your identity, or both. Inevitably this dynamic leads to stress, burnout, and even mental health issues. This not only impacts your work but also your life. If our life is made up of a series of moments then every moment spent in stress and worry is adding up to an entire life lived that way, and the negative effects bleed into other domains including our personal relationships, health, and general wellbeing. Many times, I can recall being trapped in a spiral of defeat where my every action seemed to be blocked, causing me to question myself, resulting in bad decisions and even more frustration. It may have started at work but then I took it home too in the form of low mood and distraction, thereby casting a shadow on time spent with my family. Pretty quickly a couple of bad events at work had taken all the enjoyment from an entire week. Done repeatedly and you have the recipe for a life of sadness and regret. I think many people are stuck in this place.

But it doesn't have to be this way. I believe changing your perspective on failure has the potential to change your life. Imagine for a moment that you had a week where you were productive, you made progress on your goals, you learnt something along the way, you were pleasant to be around, and you couldn't wait to begin the next week. Sounds pretty good, doesn't it? I honestly think reevaluating our approach to failure can deliver that week, every week. Not only will it transform how you approach your work and life, but it will also help you achieve more.

The paradox is that embracing failure will likely mean that you get better outcomes over the long term and hence maximise your chance of success.

Change your approach and change your life

In the remainder of this book, I'm going to dive into the benefits of embracing failure, specifically how you can accelerate growth by viewing failure as feedback. You'll unlock both personal and professional growth. The early chapters will help you examine your own relationship with failure and in the later chapters we'll apply this newfound understanding to change the way you work and lead, ultimately helping others do the same.

First, we'll break free from fear by understanding how it constrains your choices and rewriting the limiting stories you tell yourself about failure. You'll learn to recognise when fear is driving your decisions and develop the awareness that makes transformation possible.

Introduction

Then we'll turn setbacks into stepping stones by treating failure as valuable feedback and focusing on what you can control. You'll discover how to extract maximum value from every failure and paradoxically achieve better results by letting go of rigid outcome expectations.

Next, we'll prioritise progress over perfection by starting before you're ready and harnessing the power of small wins. You'll build systems for consistent imperfect action that create unstoppable momentum toward your goals.

Finally, we'll explore how to balance safety and challenge in your environment by leading with vulnerability while maintaining productive tension. You'll learn to create spaces where people feel safe enough to take risks while being challenged enough to perform at their best.

By changing your approach toward failure, you'll create freedom: the freedom to take risks, pursue meaningful goals, live in accordance with your values, and *be*—without the constant pressure of external validation.

At the end of this book, it's my sincere hope that your attitude toward failure will be changed. I hope you'll go out, seek, and embrace failure—and, in turn, free yourself. Be authentic. Live your values. And create even better work.

Part I

Break free from fear

On escaping the invisible chains of failure avoidance

Fear of failure silently shapes our decisions and limits our potential more than we realise. This invisible force often looks like prudence or perfectionism but can actually steer us away from our greatest opportunities for growth and achievement.

Understanding how fear constrains your choices is the necessary first step toward transformation. You'll see the hidden cost of "playing it safe", and how avoidance behaviours limit your impact and satisfaction. Then, by examining and rewriting the stories you tell yourself about what failure means, you'll dismantle the mental barriers that keep you from taking meaningful risks.

The benefits are immediate and far-reaching: reduced anxiety about potential mistakes, greater willingness to pursue meaningful challenges, enhanced creativity when facing obstacles, and the freedom to act despite uncertainty. This fundamental shift in how you perceive failure unlocks everything that follows—from extracting value from setbacks to building momentum through action.

1.

The hidden cost of playing it safe

"He who fears being conquered is sure of defeat."
– Napoleon Bonaparte

What if the key to increasing success wasn't working harder, but worrying less? Much like the Alcoholics Anonymous programme, I think the starting point for changing our relationship with failure needs to be accepting that you've got a problem. In this first chapter, I want to talk about how fear, and our response to fear through resistance, can hold us back from delivering our best work, genuinely enjoying work, and engaging with those around us.

If you don't think you suffer from fear or resistance to failure, let me test whether this story resonates with you:

It's Sunday afternoon. You've had a good weekend, but for some reason, mid-afternoon, a dark cloud descends on your mood. It's difficult to pinpoint why, so you start thinking about it. Where does your mind go?

The first place is generally what lies in the week ahead. On Sunday afternoon, when you've spent the best part of the weekend losing touch with exactly where you are in your work, you might think: "Okay, what do I need to do next week?" Sounds like a harmless thought, but then you've started to engage your mind on what lies ahead. Not wanting to open the laptop, you simply try to organise your work and thoughts internally. Maybe you're sitting on the couch with family and friends, but your mind is distracted, thinking about what emails you need to send on Monday morning, what was in your diary when you closed the computer on Friday afternoon, or what key milestones you need to achieve in the next week or month.

Pretty soon, you've spent the best part of your Sunday afternoon thinking about work. But what are you really thinking about? You're really thinking about whether or not you're organised, whether you've got too many emails to address, whether you've got too many meetings in your diary, whether you can actually deliver your objectives for the week. And why does this give you a negative emotional reaction? I would argue it's because you have some fear that you're not going to be able to achieve everything you want to achieve, and you're probably fearful of what others may think. Ultimately, you fear failing, either on small tasks, such as the completion of an activity, or on large milestones. And if you fail, what will others think? What will be the impact on your job? What could be the potential impact on your family?

Although these things might not be consciously recognised on the couch on a Sunday afternoon, they are at the base of your rumination, and the net impact is they have robbed you of your Sunday afternoon and probably done nothing to make you more effective in the week ahead. In fact, it may result in you entering the week with a negative view—you may be reactionary when a more thoughtful approach would get a better result. This sensation is quite common, sometimes called the "Sunday scaries". Usually assumed to occur just because the weekend is over, I think the root is fear and just one demonstration of how fear of failure is pervasive, hidden beneath the surface but impacting our everyday life. And how our response to that fear, being resistant, can prevent us from enjoying our work and from learning and improving. I can only tell this story because I suffer from it myself.

So, I want to invite you to think about another way: what if we were able to change our relationship to failure such that it's not feared? If we remove the fear from failure and approach the week ahead—or our work more generally—as a process or activity with less negative emotion, I believe the door can be opened to far greater impact and satisfaction from our work.

When fear helps and when it harms

Let's start with understanding where this fear of failure comes from. Not only is there a cultural obsession with success that makes us fear failure irrationally, but there are also more primitive and evolutionary reasons that fear may be getting in our way.

Fear is a deeply ingrained survival mechanism that has been essential to our human evolution, so it really is no wonder that we are so attached to it. Our brains are biologically wired to scan for threats and respond to danger with a fight, flight, or freeze reaction. This process is driven by the amygdala, a small but powerful part of the brain responsible for processing emotions like fear. When the brain perceives a threat, whether real or imagined, the amygdala sends a signal, triggering the release of stress hormones such as adrenaline and cortisol. This prepares the body to react quickly: your heart rate increases to pump more blood to muscles, your breathing quickens to supply oxygen, and nonessential functions like digestion slow down.

In times gone by, it's easy to see how this biological response was critical for survival. Facing a sabre-toothed tiger or a rival tribe meant life-or-death decisions, so fear kept us alert and ready to act. Fear still has a place in modern society—you really should fear if a car jumps the pavement and heads straight toward you. Those split seconds in reaction time that the adrenaline and cortisol provide could save your life.

But in today's world, the threats we face are quite different, particularly in the modern workplace. Things like failing on a project, getting negative feedback, or missing a deadline are rarely life-threatening, but it seems our brains may not easily be able to distinguish between physical danger and what could be considered mere psychological discomfort. It is said that the amygdala can react just as strongly to things like an impending presentation as it would to a predator, triggering a cascade of stress responses that are probably disproportionate to the actual risk. This can leave us feeling anxious, overwhelmed, and unable to perform at our best.

Fear doesn't just cause stress; it undermines our best efforts. This whole biological reaction has the intention of short-circuiting rational thinking. The purpose is to make you react rather than think, so it's easy to see how this response may not be the best in the workplace. If you're sitting in a meeting and hearing harsh feedback, your best approach probably isn't to react and shout down that feedback, but rather to sit there, listen, avoid defensiveness, and calmly process the information. Even if the feedback is wrong, your best response is probably going to be the result of consideration rather than immediate reaction.

1. The hidden cost of playing it safe

The psychologist Daniel Goleman coined the term "amygdala hijack" to describe how emotional responses like fear can overpower rational thought. And the cost of this over-response isn't just poor decision-making. Unchecked fear in the modern workplace also leads to:

- **Avoidance of challenges:** Fear of failure often causes us to avoid tasks entirely for the risk that they may fail.

- **Overwork and perfectionism:** In response to fear, many people compensate by overworking, reviewing every detail excessively, or avoiding delegation.

- **Reduced creativity and innovation:** These require risk-taking, and in an environment where you're trying to avoid failure at all costs, there is absolutely no room for taking on additional risk. This suppresses divergent thinking and the ability to creatively explore multiple solutions.

If you are a leader then these impacts are not just personal—they are likely influencing everything from the way you interact, to the words you choose, to the way you respond to feedback. Without awareness your own fear could be determining your management style, effectiveness, and culture within your team or organisation.

Unlearning the fear response

While our biological fear response has been essential to human survival, fear of failure itself is not something we're born with. Unlike our instinctive reactions to physical threats, fear of failure is a learnt response—shaped by our experiences, reinforced by social norms, and accumulated over time through interactions with family, education systems, and society at large.

This distinction becomes clear when we observe how children naturally approach learning and discovery. Watch a toddler learning to walk; they fall down dozens of times each day, yet they keep doing it. There's no embarrassment or concern about "doing it wrong", and certainly no anxiety about whether they're progressing at the right pace compared to other children. They simply get up and try again, focused entirely on where they are going next. Children drawing or painting demonstrate the same behaviour. Give a four- or five-year-old some pencils and paper and they instantly set to work without worrying about whether something is the wrong colour or doesn't look to be in the correct proportion—they just enjoy the process itself and proudly present their creation without fear of judgement or critique. To them it is just a picture of a dinosaur or a house, not a statement of success or failure.

This natural, fearless approach to learning stands in stark contrast to how many of us function as adults. Somewhere along the way, we've learnt to approach new challenges not with curiosity and openness, but with anxiety about potential failure. We become hyperaware of how others might judge us, paralysed by the possibility of making mistakes, and fixated on outcomes rather than enjoying the process.

I experienced this transformation firsthand when I moved to Seville for six months in my late twenties to learn Spanish. As a methodical learner, I excelled at grammar exercises and reading comprehension; activities I could perfect in private. But when it came to actually speaking Spanish with locals, I found myself terrified. What if my accent was terrible? What if I used the wrong tense? What if they laughed at my mistakes? This fear created a painful challenge: I needed to practise speaking to improve, yet my fear of speaking poorly prevented that very practice. It was only when I observed Spanish children speaking that I noticed how different their approach was. Initially I marvelled at how fluent they were, despite their years, and found a new reason to be hard on myself. But then I noticed the mistakes they made—incorrect word choice, mixing up their verbs, sentences that didn't make sense. The only difference was that they showed no sign of fear or embarrassment, they just continued chatting away, sometimes with gentle correction from their parents which was also simply incorporated without hesitation. They hadn't learnt to fear failure yet.

I had the same experience when I learnt to play the piano as an adult. I'd diligently practise scales and simple pieces, in private, on my own, but I'd refuse to play for anyone else. The thought of fumbling the keys and playing at the standard of a five-year-old filled me with dread. By contrast my son, who just started learning the piano, took part in a small concert that his teacher organised. He could not wait to get up on stage and play the grand piano for everyone and wasn't worried at all that he might play his piece wrong.

These experiences revealed something profound: my fear of failure wasn't an inherent part of learning—it was a learnt response. Somewhere between childhood and adulthood, I had absorbed the message that mistakes reflect poorly on my intelligence, competence, and worth. I had internalised the idea that learning should happen in private until perfection is achieved, rather than seeing the messy process of learning as natural and necessary.

Understanding that fear of failure is learnt rather than innate offers hope. Just as we've learnt this fear, we can unlearn it.

The success trap

Fear is something that needs to be managed generally, but with respect to failure, there is another interesting phenomenon: high achievers often suffer from this dynamic even more. Those who are seeking success, who are celebrated for their drive, their relentless pursuit, or their perfectionism, may ironically be more vulnerable to anxiety and fear of failure.

Ora Aarons-Mele explains in *The Anxious Achiever* that these individuals are particularly prone to thought traps, or ingrained ways of thinking that heighten fear and undermine confidence. These thought traps include:

- **All-or-nothing thinking:** Viewing situations in extremes: if it's not perfect, it's a disaster. For example, when you deliver a presentation and make one small mistake, you may conclude the whole thing was a failure.
- **Catastrophising:** Jumping to the worst-case scenario without evidence. Aarons-Mele uses the example of a lawyer who imagined being sued for malpractice and compulsively rechecked his work, even on vacation.
- **Social comparison:** Comparing yourself unfavourably to others, assuming that everyone else has it together. This is even more heightened in the modern era of social media where every action needs to be reported to the world at large.
- **Labelling:** Personalising external events or internalising failure as a personal defect: "Something I did failed, so I am a failure."

1. The hidden cost of playing it safe

These thought traps hold high achievers back. They generally result in diminished performance as high achievers overwork to the point of not being productive, seek perfectionism to the extent of producing nothing, or avoid work or activities entirely.

And then there's the health toll. Putting together the biological reaction we discussed, where brain chemicals intended for occasional use are being produced on a regular basis to increase physical reactions like heart rate and breathing, it's easy to see how fear results in chronic anxiety and can manifest in burnout, sleep problems, and other health issues.

Fear served a purpose for early humans but needs to be rethought in the modern workplace. Unfortunately, those who are seeking success most are probably at the greatest risk of the fear of failure impacting their overall achievement.

Stop fighting, start accepting

Sometimes I think the fun has been taken out of work by the numerous rules that have developed on what is and isn't acceptable. One such example is a lesson I learnt at a management retreat many years ago. The method would likely not be acceptable now, but the lesson remains.

It was an afternoon session, immediately after lunch, when a very solidly built executive called for volunteers. Naturally, none came forward, preferring to sit in the audience and digest slowly. But unfortunately, I was sitting in the front row, so I got called up. What came next was the unusual part.

Without any context being explained, he told me he was going to shoulder charge me. Naturally, I braced, and he charged his immense weight directly into my shoulder. I sort of bounced off him, both in immense pain and also wondering what the point of this exercise could possibly be. I was even more horrified to learn that the embarrassment would go on as he demanded that I then shoulder charge him. As a dutiful junior professional, I did, but what he did at that point was commence motion in the same direction so as to take away the moment of impact, and we kind of fell to a heap on the floor.

After collecting ourselves, he finally made his point. When I braced against the oncoming force, there was immense pain. But when he accepted what was coming and went in the same direction, there was no pain. The lesson was to identify when you were fighting something and when you should go with it for a better outcome. Perhaps the clumsiest management retreat exercise I have ever done, but it certainly made it memorable.

Our reaction to fear is the same. When we see something bad coming, either actually or mentally, we brace for impact or avoid it which brings about pain. The trouble is that we are reacting to an emotion or an imagined future pain that may or may not occur. The only certainty is that we will experience the pain of resistance right now.

The concept of resistance being at the root of all pain is not just taught in management theory. It's been central to Buddhist philosophy for hundreds of years, particularly in the teachings around suffering. The essence is simple, yet profound. The pain is inevitable, but the suffering is optional.

What this means is that pain comes from setbacks, failures, or discomfort—things we cannot control. The suffering, on the other hand, comes from our resistance to these experiences. When we refuse to accept reality for what it is and cling to expectations of how things should be instead of what they are, we create tension which intensifies the pain of failure.

The Buddhists often describe this concept as the "second arrow". The first arrow is the actual pain or failure. This will happen as there's always pain from failure. But the second arrow is the suffering we create through resistance: the rumination, anger, and self-blame or fear that comes from the failure.

Resistance usually comes in one of three forms:

1. **Refusal to accept reality:** This happens when expectations clash with reality. For example, a new business founder may expect their company to scale quickly, but market conditions slow progress. Instead of accepting the setback, they deny it, overextend resources, or blame others, therefore worsening the situation.
2. **Clinging to unrealistic expectations:** Our society fuels the illusion that we can control outcomes and that success is limitless. When reality falls short, we resist it by blaming ourselves, others, or external circumstances.
3. **Fighting past events:** Resistance to failure often means mentally revisiting it repeatedly, unable to let go. This rumination prevents learning and creates prolonged emotional suffering. How many times, for example, have you replayed a presentation that may not have gone well? The initial pain comes immediately after the presentation when perhaps you haven't got your message across effectively. But resisting the fact that it happened, looking for external

reasons why the failure occurred, or constantly going over what could have been different means you don't take the lessons forward and simply extend the suffering.

Fear and resistance combined increase mental stress and reduce performance. And these aren't just abstract barriers; they have a real and measurable impact on our personal and professional lives. Left unchecked, they create a cycle of stress, poor performance, and dissatisfaction that holds us back from achieving our full potential. The costs of fear and resistance can include:

- **Stress and burnout:** Fear of failure keeps us on edge, constantly scanning for threats. Resistance makes us mentally replay failures, amplifying their emotional impact. The result is chronic stress.

- **Reduced creativity and innovation:** Fear narrows our focus to avoid failure rather than exploring opportunities. Resistance prevents us from seeing failure as data or a chance to learn and iterate. It's well known that companies with risk-averse cultures fail to innovate because leaders resist uncomfortable realities and fear taking bold action.

- **Missed opportunities for growth:** When fear and resistance drive our decisions, we avoid challenges, risks, and feedback—the very things we need to grow. An anxious executive who avoids public speaking opportunities, for example, denies themselves the chance to improve their leadership impact.

- **Lower work satisfaction and happiness:** Living in constant fear of failure or denial of setbacks creates a sense of helplessness and dissatisfaction. It erodes our confidence, drains our energy, and steals the joy from work. Happy professionals are those who accept failure as part of the process and focus on progress, not perfection.

Freedom through radical acceptance

Just as fear and resistance create unnecessary suffering, acceptance offers a pathway to freedom. Not the passive acceptance of defeat, but what psychologists call "radical acceptance", a profound acknowledgement of reality that allows us to respond effectively rather than react emotionally.

Think about how differently two professionals might handle a critical presentation that goes poorly. The first spends weeks replaying every mistake, agonising over what others think, and letting the experience erode their confidence. The second acknowledges the reality—yes, it didn't go well but quickly shifts focus to learning and improving. Same event, radically different impact. This distinction between pain and suffering that we discussed earlier becomes crucial here. The presentation's outcome might cause momentary pain for both individuals—that's natural and inevitable. But the first person's resistance creates ongoing suffering while the second person's acceptance allows them to move forward productively.

What makes acceptance so powerful is how it frees up mental and emotional resources. When we stop expending energy fighting reality or resisting what has already happened, we can direct that energy toward learning and growth. It's like the difference between swimming against a current versus working with it to reach your destination.

The practice of acceptance operates on three levels:

1. **Factual acceptance:** This means acknowledging what has actually happened without sugar-coating or catastrophising. A project failed. A deadline was missed. A client was lost. Simple, unvarnished reality.

2. **Emotional acceptance:** This involves allowing ourselves to feel whatever emotions arise without judgement or resistance. Disappointment, frustration, embarrassment—these feelings are all valid parts of the experience.

3. **Functional acceptance:** This is about recognising what aspects of the situation we can and cannot control, then focusing our energy on what's within our influence.

The benefits of this approach extend far beyond stress reduction. Research reveals a cascading effect of acceptance on professional performance. Teams and individuals who practise acceptance demonstrate remarkable resilience, bouncing back from setbacks with greater speed and adaptability. They also show enhanced learning capacity, drawing deeper insights from their failures rather than becoming defensive or discouraged.

This acceptance-based mindset creates the psychological safety needed for intelligent risk-taking. When people aren't paralysed by fear of failure, they make bolder moves while maintaining good judgement. Their professional relationships tend to be stronger too, built on authentic communication rather than defensive posturing.

Perhaps most significantly, acceptance fosters innovation and creativity. When minds aren't preoccupied with avoiding failure or maintaining appearances, they're free to explore new possibilities and generate novel solutions. It's the difference between an executive who demands perfect plans before acting and one who encourages thoughtful experimentation and learning.

Failure can be accepted too

Our relationship with failure lies at the heart of this dynamic between fear, resistance, and acceptance. Most professionals spend enormous energy trying to avoid failure, creating elaborate defence mechanisms that ultimately hold them back from their full potential. We brace against it like I braced against that shoulder charge—and like that exercise demonstrated, our resistance often causes more pain than the impact itself.

Think about how this plays out in your own life. How many Sunday afternoons have you wasted worrying about potential failure in the week ahead? How many opportunities have you declined before even exploring them because you have already decided that the risk of humiliation or being exposed is too great? Can you possibly be creative if you are constantly trying to avoid any risk of an incorrect choice? And the cost isn't just in wasted time or potential. It affects everything you do or don't do, your emotional state, your relationships, and your personal wellbeing.

But there is another way: radical acceptance. When we open ourselves to the possibility of failure, and even plan for it, something amazing happens. Suddenly failure isn't something to be avoided, it is something to be learnt from; it's information we are seeking rather than something we are avoiding. Of course, the pain doesn't disappear entirely, and nor should it as disappointment is feedback too. It's valuable information that can inform our next choice and move us forward to a new destination, only visible because of the steps before and only because resistance and rumination didn't prevent us from embarking on the journey.

The benefits of this shift in mindset are not limited to receiving more feedback and information. You'll also make better decisions. When we're not distracted by fear, or by finding reasons things may fail, we free our mental energy and focus to clearly observe what is real and make rational assessments and judgements. We're also free to explore more creative answers to problems and challenges if we accept the potential that any single choice may result in disappointment, which we will understand and carry on anyway. It is this change in relationship to failure that results in the ultimate paradox: that accepting failure makes us more likely to succeed.

The rest of this book will help you make this transformation. You'll learn to recognise when a fear of failure is driving your behaviour, how this learnt response may be informing how you view the world, and how to turn resistance and suffering into feedback and information. Importantly, we'll explore concrete tools and techniques you can leverage every day to accept failure as a reality without feeling like you are lowering your standards or simply submitting to defeat. The promise is simple: by changing your relationship with failure, you'll free yourself to do your best work. The only thing that will be released is a psychological burden, not your commitment to excellence or success, as you'll learn that these outcomes are often the result of setbacks or even numerous setbacks along the way. The difference is that you can release your fear to enjoy the journey, be fully present to engage in every moment, and even help others do the same. Success will come not from avoiding failure, but from fearlessly accepting it.

In the next chapter, we'll begin this transformation by examining the powerful stories we tell ourselves about failure. These narratives—often unconscious but deeply influential—shape everything from our daily decisions to our long-term aspirations. By understanding and reshaping these stories, we take the first step toward a healthier, more productive relationship with failure.

Key takeaways

- Recognise when fear is driving your decisions by noticing physical symptoms (like Sunday night anxiety) or avoidance behaviours that keep you "safely" away from risks.

- Distinguish between productive fear (which protects you from genuine threats) and destructive fear (which prevents growth) by asking: "Is this keeping me safe or keeping me small?"

- Break the cycle of resistance by accepting temporary discomfort rather than fighting against it, which only amplifies anxiety and creates additional suffering.

- Practise radical acceptance of what you cannot control while redirecting energy toward what you can influence to transform paralysing fear into focused action.

- Counteract the high achiever's vulnerability to fear by actively acknowledging that perfectionism and excessive self-criticism are obstacles to performance, not drivers of it.

2.

Choose a better story

"Whether you think you can, or think you can't, you're right."
– Henry Ford

Standing before Stanford's graduating class of 2005, Steve Jobs made a surprising confession: "Getting fired from Apple was the best thing that could have ever happened to me." It was a statement that perfectly captured the complex nature of success and failure—how a potentially career-ending moment could become the catalyst for unprecedented achievement. How, regarded as a setback, that moment led to ultimate success.

Steve Jobs' life really does read like a modern Greek epic with many rises and falls, moments of remarkable achievement, and then significant missteps. In so many ways he is the perfect case study in how perspective shapes our view of success and failure. How snapshots taken from different points in time, by different observers, using different measures, can lead to vastly different conclusions.

Born in 1955, and adopted at birth, Jobs' early life perhaps foreshadowed his later pattern of unconventional choices and spirituality. His college years at Reed exemplified his tendency to change direction and follow his intuition—after one semester studying toward a major in English literature, he dropped out of the formal programme, choosing instead to sleep on friends' floors and attend classes that sparked his curiosity. Among these was a calligraphy course that would seem to have no practical value for either a literature major or a technology enthusiast.

In 1974, Jobs took a turn away from his career pursuit altogether, travelling to India in search of spiritual enlightenment. He spent seven months studying Buddhism, experiencing diverse cultures, seeking guidance from spiritual teachers and returned with a shaved head, wearing traditional Indian clothing, having embraced Buddhist principles that would influence his thinking throughout his life. He also observed extreme poverty in India, which he later credited with shaping his minimalist design philosophy and focus on simplicity.

Upon his return, Jobs continued his spiritual journey, practising Zen Buddhism under Kōun Yamada. He maintained a lifelong meditation practice and attributed much of his success to his ability to focus and find clarity through meditation. This spiritual dimension might seem at odds with his later reputation as a hard-driving business leader, yet it profoundly influenced his approach to product design and his vision of technology's role in human life.

Given his previous few years, it seems unlikely then that in 1976 he would co-found Apple Computer with Steve Wozniak from his garage in California. Whilst initial products like the Apple I and Apple II achieved moderate success (I certainly loved playing the Carmen Sandiego detective game at school), it was the Macintosh that truly demonstrated Jobs' vision of user-friendly computing. And yet in 1985, just one year after its release, he was forced out the very company he had founded, following a power struggle with the board and CEO John Sculley.

2. Choose a better story

The next phase of Jobs' career shows that inclination to pursue multiple paths at the same time when he founded NeXT Computer and also acquired Pixar. NeXT produced expensive, sophisticated workstations that never achieved commercial success. Pixar was originally a hardware company selling high-end graphics computers and it was struggling when acquired from George Lucas for $10 million in 1986. In fact, the bleed of cash was such that Jobs initially needed to invest millions of his own money to keep it going before pivoting into animation software and finally film making, ultimately becoming the company famed for blockbuster animations that we identify today. But it was NeXT that paved the way for Jobs' rise to fame when Apple acquired the company for $429 million in 1996 and brought him back as an advisor. This new era didn't begin well, and Jobs only became CEO in 1997 when the company was facing imminent bankruptcy, but it is under his leadership that we see the first groundbreaking products appear including the iPod. What followed was one of the most amazing turnarounds in corporate history as Apple moved from product success to product success, revolutionising multiple industries with innovations like the iMac, iPhone, and iPad. Each new product contributed to Apple's change in direction from computers to consumer electronics and in the end to one of the world's most valuable companies.

Jobs passed away from pancreatic cancer in 2011 and is generally associated with a halo of success and innovation, but I think his complex legacy can be viewed through quite different lenses.

The Failure Perspective: Jobs' life from the outset could be seen as a series of significant failures. Dropping out of classes and then of school entirely is generally frowned upon. His indulgent spiritual seeking, interest in Eastern philosophy, and time spent meditating delayed his real work. Then when he got to work it seems his perfectionism and demanding nature strained relationships and meant he didn't get on with his colleagues leading to the ousting from one company, the need to pour millions into another, and then the commercial failure of NeXT. Even late in his life he rejected conventional medical treatment for his cancer in favour of unconventional medicines, a decision that left doctors confounded and some say cost him his life. His management style was always controversial being variously described as anything from perfectionistic to toxic.

The Success Perspective: Seen a different way, Jobs' journey can be seen as the rise of one of the most successful innovators and businesspeople history has ever seen. The intellectual curiosity that saw him change courses and seek spiritual enlightenment saw him develop a unique perspective on design that would revolutionise products. That time spent studying calligraphy went on to Apple changing the game with its revolutionary typography and attention to aesthetic detail. Many credit him with transforming no less than six industries: personal computing, animated movies, music, phones, tablet computing, and digital publishing. Apple went from near bankruptcy to becoming the world's most valuable company. Pixar was sold to Disney for $7.4 billion. NeXT even developed the technology that would become the foundation of Apple's iOS and OSX operating systems. Even his ousting from Apple allowed him to develop new perspectives on the market and return with greater wisdom and experience to take the company to new heights.

The events themselves don't change—what changes is the story we tell about them. Jobs' greatest triumph may have been his ability to see supposed failures not as endpoints but as plot turns in a larger narrative of innovation and discovery. His Stanford speech wasn't just about getting fired; it was about how getting fired freed him to "enter one of the most creative periods" of his life.

In the end, Jobs' life serves as a powerful reminder that success and failure often aren't opposite outcomes, but rather different interpretations of the same events. The key lies not in what happens to us, but in how we choose to interpret and learn from those experiences.

Stories shape everything

The dual interpretations of Steve Jobs' life illustrate a fundamental truth about human nature: we are, at our core, storytellers. The raw facts of Jobs' journey—college dropout, fired executive, failed products—could be assembled into either triumph or tragedy. What matters most is not the events themselves, but the meaning we extract from them.

This human drive to find meaning runs far deeper than simple preference. It is, as cognitive scientists and philosophers have discovered, fundamental to how we process and understand the world around us. Perhaps no one understood this better than Viktor Frankl, whose insights into human meaning-making emerged from the darkest possible circumstances—the Nazi concentration camps.

Frankl, an Austrian psychiatrist, lost everything in those camps: his parents, his wife, his unborn child, and every material possession. Yet in this crucible of suffering, he made an extraordinary observation. The survivors weren't necessarily the physically strongest or the most practical. Instead, those who endured often had something less tangible but infinitely more powerful: a sense of meaning that transcended their immediate circumstances.

Frankl himself found purpose in imagining a future where he would teach others about the psychological insights he was gaining. In a moment of clarity amid unimaginable horror, he realised that while he couldn't control what happened to him, he could control the story he told about those events—and through that story, find the strength to continue. But his insights appeared not just from his personal survival but also from systematic observations as both a prisoner and a psychiatrist in the camps. He noticed striking patterns among his fellow prisoners. Some who appeared physically robust would surrender to despair and die within days, while others who seemed much weaker physically would demonstrate remarkable resilience. The key difference, he discovered, lay not in their physical condition or even their circumstances, but in their ability to maintain a sense of meaning through the stories they told themselves about their experience.

Through his observations, Frankl found three primary ways that people found meaning, even in the most horrific conditions: through purposeful work (even if merely helping fellow prisoners), through love (holding onto connections with absent loved ones), and through suffering itself—finding purpose in the very act of enduring with dignity. These weren't merely coping mechanisms; they were different narrative frameworks that transformed identical circumstances into entirely different lived experiences.

In his seminal work *Man's Search for Meaning*, Frankl wrote, "Everything can be taken from a man but one thing: the last of

2. Choose a better story

human freedoms—to choose one's attitude in any given set of circumstances, to choose one's own way." This wasn't philosophical abstraction—it was a truth proven repeatedly in the camps. Prisoners who could maintain a story of purpose, whether it was reuniting with loved ones or completing unfinished work, showed dramatically higher survival rates than those who lost their sense of meaning.

This understanding of narrative's power to shape not just our experience but our very survival has been reinforced by subsequent research. Studies in fields from medicine to athletics have shown that the stories we tell about our circumstances profoundly influence our physiological responses, immune function, and performance outcomes. When patients view illness as a "challenge" rather than a "threat", they show better recovery rates. When athletes frame anxiety as "excitement" rather than "fear", their performance improves.

I think this same principle applies to our relationship with failure. Just as Frankl's fellow prisoners faced identical circumstances, but experienced them differently based on their internal narratives, I've seen how different individuals can face similar setbacks yet emerge with vastly different outcomes based on the stories they tell themselves about failure. Some people seem to collapse in the face of minor adversity and others seem to be able to dust themselves off and carry on.

A prime example in the corporate world is how people approach restructuring and lay-offs. This may seem trivial when set alongside Frankl's experience in prison camps but people facing the prospect of losing their way of life, not being able to support their families, and an uncertain future can face similar emotions.

Working in business transformation I have been part of many business reorganisations where people are faced with unemployment due to factors entirely outside of their control and I have found the range of reactions to be astounding. Initial shock is somewhat universal, but the paths diverge from there. Some people quickly move to appreciation for a modest lump sum of cash and the freedom to explore new paths. Others, even with objectively better prospects, seem to wallow in self-doubt, what could have been done differently, and fail to move forward.

Five failure fallacies

But what is the "right story" to choose? Continuing with Frankl's experience, the right stories were those that allowed people to carry on, to make progress, and live another day. Very simply, they chose helpful stories rather than unhelpful stories. Based on my own experience and working with other anxious achievers, I've identified five common failure fallacies I think we need to overcome. These are flawed patterns of thinking that damage our outlook and, if corrected, could reshape our relationship with setbacks from one of fear to one of opportunity.

Fallacy 1: There is one single truth

In offices around the world business leaders pore over spreadsheets and slide decks, seeking what they believe to be the objective truth. "The numbers don't lie," they say, or "Let's stick to the facts." This devotion to data reflects a deeply held belief, and trained practice, that somewhere beneath the complexity and chaos of the world lies an indisputable reality waiting to be discovered. But does it really?

This pursuit of absolute truth isn't new. In fact, it's a philosophical debate that has gone on for centuries, one that goes to the heart of how we know what we know. On one side stand the rationalists led by thinkers like René Descartes (who famously declared: "I think, therefore I am.") for whom truth emerges not from what we observe, but from what we can reason. Just as mathematical principles exist independent of human observation, they argued, certain fundamental truths await discovery through pure logical deduction.

On the opposite side stand the empiricists, championed by the likes of John Locke and David Hume, who insisted that all knowledge flows from experience. Locke saw the human mind as a "blank slate" at birth, gradually filled through observation and experience. Hume extended this idea even further, questioning whether we can truly know anything beyond what we directly experience. Even our belief in cause and effect, he argued, stems not from logic but from habit—from seeing the same patterns repeat until we assume they must continue.

To provide a simple illustration of these two views, imagine you are sitting at your desk in the office and hear a door slamming shut. The empiricist might assume a simple chain of physical events: an open window, a gust of wind, a change in air pressure, and the resulting slam. No judgement or prior experience enters the interpretation, just a sequence of physical events. The rationalist, drawing on experience and logical deduction, might interpret the same event as an expression of an employee's frustration, seeing the slammed door as part of a pattern of workplace tension. Both interpretations could be valid. Both could contain truth. And herein lies the challenge for modern business: we are trained to seek singular objective truths when reality often presents us with multiple valid interpretations of the same events.

This philosophical tension plays out daily in business decisions. When a product fails in the market, is it because of measurable factors like price point and feature set (the empiricist view), or does it reflect deeper truths about human psychology and social trends (the rationalist perspective)? When an employee leaves, does exit interview data tell the whole story, or do we need to reason beyond the observable facts to understand the true causes? Countless hours are spent on questions like these, trying to find the single answer, when in reality either or both could be true.

Hume advised: "A wise man proportions his belief to the evidence." But perhaps modern business wisdom requires us to go further and recognise that evidence itself can be interpreted in multiple ways, and that truth often lies not in choosing between rational deduction and empirical observation, but in understanding how both approaches illuminate different aspects of reality.

This insight has profound implications for our relationship with failure—if we open ourselves to the possibility that multiple valid interpretations can coexist, we can fundamentally change how we approach setbacks and challenges. Instead of seeing failure as a fixed, singular truth, we can recognise it as one perspective among many possible interpretations. This shift from absolute to multiple truths turns failure from a predetermined destination into a space of possibilities.

Consider how differently we might approach a challenging project if we abandon the belief in a single truth. Rather than seeing only two possible outcomes, success or failure, we become open to multiple pathways and interpretations. This multiplicity of truth doesn't mean abandoning critical thinking or accountability, but rather it means approaching failure with curiosity rather than dread. When we understand that no single interpretation holds a monopoly on truth, we free ourselves to explore setbacks with genuine interest. What else might this mean? What other possibilities does this open up? What alternative perspectives might reveal new opportunities?

Fallacy 2: Our judgements are unbiased

The debate between rationalists and empiricists highlights how different lenses can lead to different truths, but there's an even more subtle force at work in how we interpret events: the unconscious biases that colour our perception before we even begin to reason or observe. Like a filter on a camera lens, these biases shape our view of reality without our awareness, particularly when it comes to understanding failure. Imagine standing in front of a mirror that subtly distorts your reflection—not enough to be immediately obvious, but perhaps enough to subconsciously change how you see yourself. Our cognitive biases work in much the same way, warping our perception of events in predictable patterns that can profoundly affect the stories we tell ourselves about failure.

Consider confirmation bias, perhaps the most insidious of these distortions. Like a selective listener who only hears what they expect to hear, confirmation bias causes us to embrace information that supports our existing beliefs while dismissing evidence that challenges them. A person who deeply believes they aren't cut out for leadership might receive a performance review containing both praise and criticism. Despite an equal balance of positive and negative feedback, they'll likely remember and dwell on the criticisms while barely registering the compliments. The story they tell themselves—"I'm not a good leader"—becomes a self-fulfilling prophecy, not because it's true, but because they're unconsciously filtering reality to support it.

Then there's negativity bias, the tendency to give more weight to negative experiences than positive. Consider a musician who performs ten songs flawlessly but makes a single mistake in the eleventh. Hours later, lying awake in bed, which moment do you think plays on repeat in their mind? Negativity bias ensures that one wrong note drowns out an ocean of right ones, distorting the story of the performance from triumph to tragedy.

Perhaps most interesting in the context of failure is the self-serving bias, which acts like a mental accountant who keeps two sets of books: one for our successes, which we claim as personal achievements, and another for our failures, which we attribute to external circumstances. A project fails, and suddenly we become master storytellers, weaving tales about insufficient resources, unsupportive colleagues, or impossible deadlines. While these external factors might indeed play a role, the self-serving bias prevents us from seeing, and learning from, our own contributions to the outcome. Think of a tennis player who wins a match and proudly declares: "I played really well today," but after losing explains: "The sun was in my eyes, and the court surface was uneven." Same player, same skills, but two very different stories depending on the outcome. This selective attribution doesn't just protect our ego; it robs us of valuable opportunities for growth and learning.

Once we recognise how these unconscious filters distort our perception, we can begin to question the stories we tell ourselves about failure. Was that project really a complete disaster, or is negativity bias amplifying the setbacks while minimising the successes? Are we truly victims of circumstance, or is self-serving bias preventing us from seeing our role in the outcome? Is our belief about our abilities based on objective evidence, or has confirmation bias curated a highlight reel of our worst moments?

The power of these biases lies in their invisibility. Like a fish unaware of the water it swims in, we rarely notice how these mental shortcuts shape our interpretation of events. But unlike the fish, we have the capacity to recognise and adjust for these distortions. By understanding our cognitive biases, we can begin to see our failures, and ourselves, more clearly, free from the unconscious filters that so often turn temporary setbacks into permanent personal narratives.

Fallacy 3: Failure is final

Nothing generates fear like the belief that failure is final and there can be no recovery. This finality means that sometimes we don't even embark on the journey and explore the potential because the outcome is inevitable and final. I find this fallacy manifests for people in two ways: those who believe failure to be a permanent state that cannot be altered and those who continually raise the bar of performance such that they will always fall short.

The first can be described as the defeatist narrative where we transform temporary setbacks into permanent declarations of inadequacy. A talented programmer encounters a bug that can't be immediately solved, and suddenly the story becomes: "I'll never be good enough for this field." A promising entrepreneur faces their first failed venture, and the narrative shifts to: "I'm not cut out for business." Each setback isn't seen as a learning opportunity but as confirmation of an underlying fatal flaw. These defeatist stories are particularly dangerous because they masquerade as wisdom or self-protection. "Why try again if I'm just going to fail?" sounds like prudent risk assessment, but it's actually a narrative prison, keeping its inhabitants safely—and permanently—confined within the walls of their own fears.

The other form is the perfectionist narrative which actually creates failure out of what many would consider to be a good result. A student receives an A- and spends hours agonising over the few points lost rather than celebrating their mastery of the material. An executive successfully leads a major project but fixates on the one deadline that slipped by two days, weaving a story of inadequacy from threads of nearly universal success. Perfectionist narratives are particularly cruel because they deny even the possibility of satisfaction. Every victory becomes tainted, every success incomplete. It's like trying to reach the horizon, no matter how far you walk, it remains eternally out of reach. The story becomes not one of progress and achievement, but of perpetually falling short.

Both narratives, defeatist and perfectionist, share a common downside: they prevent growth by making failure too significant. The defeatist makes failure final ("Why bother trying again?"), while the perfectionist makes it unacceptable ("Nothing less than perfection will do"). Both stories trap their believers in cycles of anxiety, self-doubt, and missed opportunities.

A more productive narrative might view failure as information rather than indictment, as temporary rather than permanent, as specific rather than universal. The bug in the code becomes not proof of incompetence but a puzzle to be solved. The failed venture becomes not a final verdict but a costly and valuable education in business. These healthier narratives remain grounded in reality. They don't deny the existence of failure or its emotional impact, but they create space for growth, learning, and future success. They acknowledge the pain of falling short while maintaining the possibility of future achievement.

The choice of narrative becomes particularly crucial because it often creates self-fulfilling prophecies. Tell yourself that failure is final, and you'll likely stop trying. Convince yourself that anything less than perfection is worthless, and you'll rarely find the courage to begin. But craft a story that views failure as a necessary step toward mastery, and suddenly every setback becomes a building block rather than a roadblock. In the end, the most dangerous thing about these limiting narratives is not that they're false—it's that they become true through our belief in them.

Fallacy 4: I failed so I am a failure

Let me illustrate this one with a personal example that sticks in my mind. Picture a familiar scene in consulting: a team of bright minds locked in a room, surrounded by whiteboards covered in diagrams and bullet points, all focused on solving a client's pressing problem. In this case, we were tackling workplace safety, a challenge that literally meant life or death. After hours of intense discussion and analysis, we believed we had cracked it. The solution seemed perfect, elegant even. We left that evening feeling the unique satisfaction that comes from solving a complex puzzle.

The next day's client presentation remains etched in my memory, but not for the reasons we had anticipated. As we confidently laid out our solution, the client began methodically dismantling it.

Point by point, they presented evidence that revealed the flaws in our thinking. They weren't being hostile; they were simply right. What happened next reveals a crucial truth about how we handle failure. Instead of accepting the feedback gracefully, we became defensive. We argued back, making increasingly weak counter-points. Looking back, I can see that our resistance had nothing to do with the merits of our solution. It was about something much more personal: our identities had become entangled with our ideas.

This fusion of identity and outcome is one of the most dangerous traps we can fall into when dealing with failure. When we equate a failed project with personal inadequacy, we transform a simple professional setback into an existential crisis. It's the difference between "This approach didn't work" and "I am not good enough".

Consider the difference between these two internal narratives:

"I failed at this task" versus "I am a failure"

"This idea didn't work" versus "I am not smart enough"

"This attempt fell short" versus "I am inadequate"

The first statement in each pair describes an event, something that happened. The second transforms that event into an identity, something you are. This minor shift in language reflects a massive shift in meaning, turning temporary setbacks into permanent character flaws.

Thomas Edison understood this distinction intuitively. When he was faced with thousands of unsuccessful attempts to create a working light bulb, he famously declared: "I have not failed. I've just found 10,000 ways that won't work." Notice the careful separation in his words: the experiments failed, but Edison himself remained undiminished. Each unsuccessful attempt was simply data, not a referendum on his worth as an inventor or person.

Separating outcome from identity isn't just about maintaining self-esteem; it's about preserving our ability to learn and grow. When we view failure as a reflection of our identity, we become defensive, like my team arguing with our client. We fight to protect our ego rather than absorb valuable feedback and become risk-averse, avoiding situations where failure might confirm our deepest fears about ourselves.

Reflecting on that consulting engagement now, I can see how differently it could have played out. If we had truly separated our professional contribution from our personal worth, we might have responded to the client's feedback with curiosity rather than defensiveness. We could have seen their insights not as an attack on our capabilities but as valuable information that would make our next attempt more successful. The tension I felt that evening wasn't really about our failed solution—it was about the story I was telling myself about what that failure meant. By conflating a flawed idea with personal inadequacy, I had transformed a simple professional setback into a threat to my self-worth.

This pattern plays out across all domains of life. The entrepreneur whose first venture fails begins to doubt not just their business model but their ability to be an entrepreneur at all. The artist whose work is rejected starts to question not just the piece but their creative identity. The leader whose strategy doesn't succeed begins to doubt not just the plan but their capacity to lead.

The antidote to this pattern lies in consciously maintaining the boundary between what we do and who we are. This doesn't mean detaching completely from our work—passion and personal investment are valuable drivers of excellence. Rather, it means recognising that while our efforts may sometimes fall short, these outcomes don't define our worth or potential. When we can truly separate failure from identity, we free ourselves to take bolder risks, accept feedback more openly, and learn more deeply from our mistakes. We can bring our full creativity and effort to each new challenge without fearing that failure will confirm some fundamental flaw in who we are.

In the end, the most liberating truth about failure might be this: our attempts may fail, but that doesn't make us failures. Our ideas may not work, but that doesn't make us inadequate. Our projects may fall short, but we remain whole, capable, and worthy of success.

Fallacy 5: I can't admit failure

Most people believe admitting failure will damage their credibility, but I have found the opposite to be true. Particularly common in business settings, our tendency is to cover up flawed positions and mistakes or to deflect responsibility. We fear being wrong. But both research and my own experience indicate that acknowledging failure can actually enhance professional standing rather than diminish it.

My experience with the safety presentation was a case-in-point. After initially defending our weak proposal, we regrouped and eventually returned to the client acknowledging that we'd overlooked various aspects. To my surprise, the client was pleased to see we were taking their feedback on board and that we were more interested in getting the best possible outcome rather than

2. Choose a better story

being seen to be right. The whole episode ultimately served to strengthen our relationship.

Research also indicates that a key attribute of authentic leaders, the most influential, is their ability to admit when they're wrong and be open to the possibility that they don't know everything. This self-awareness and humility show a commitment to learning, over ego, and creates resonance with others that builds trust and genuine connection.

An oft-cited example of this leadership attribute in action was Howard Schultz's experience with Starbucks. In the 1980s, Starbucks faced significant challenges due to rapid expansion and deviation from its core values. The company had grown too quickly, was criticised for introducing pre-packaged foods that compromised the coffee experience, and struggled with operational issues.

Instead of defending these choices, Schultz took direct action. He wrote a memo titled "The Commoditisation of the Starbucks Experience" explicitly acknowledging where the company had gone wrong. This admission took many in the business community by surprise but became the foundation for meaningful change. Starbucks closed underperforming stores, retrained baristas, and reinvested in coffee quality and customer experience. The results were telling. Starbucks not only recovered but emerged stronger, with enhanced customer loyalty and employee engagement. Schultz's willingness to acknowledge failure strengthened rather than weakened his leadership position, demonstrating his commitment to the company's long-term success over short-term face-saving.

But you don't need case studies or psychological research to know this phenomenon to be true. I am sure you, like me, tend to trust people more when they have the ability to admit they don't have all the answers. Sure, we might expect some people to have more experience or knowledge than others on a certain topic, but it is impossible that someone will never be wrong and hence our suspicions are rightly raised when someone presents to the contrary. When leaders insist on a façade of perfection, they create distance and scepticism, and it is only by acknowledging failure and showing a willingness to learn that they can build genuine connection and trust.

The implications for professional practice are clear. The energy spent defending mistakes or maintaining appearances often does more harm than good. Real credibility comes from:

- addressing issues directly rather than hiding them
- focusing on learning and improvement
- demonstrating values through actions
- creating an environment where others feel safe acknowledging mistakes.

As organisations face increasingly complex challenges, the ability to acknowledge and learn from failure becomes essential. Leaders who understand that vulnerability can enhance credibility and gain a valuable tool for building trust and driving organisational learning.

This insight has practical applications across professional contexts. When mistakes occur, prompt acknowledgement followed by focused attention on improvement often yields better results than defensive positioning. This approach not only builds trust but also creates opportunities for genuine learning and growth. The evidence shows clearly that admitting failure, when combined with commitment to improvement, strengthens rather than weakens professional credibility. In an environment that increasingly values authenticity and transparency, the ability to acknowledge mistakes while demonstrating dedication to growth becomes a crucial professional skill.

Choose the story that empowers you

As we've explored the various fallacies about failure, the key question remains: what is the "right" story to tell? The answer begins with awareness. We must first become conscious of the stories we're currently telling ourselves about failure. Are we falling into the trap of seeing failure as final? Are we confusing a failed attempt with personal inadequacy? Are we clinging to the myth of a single, absolute truth? This awareness alone is transformative. As we saw with Viktor Frankl's observations in the concentration camps, simply recognising that we have a choice in how we interpret our circumstances can be profoundly empowering. The moment we realise we're telling ourselves a story, rather than stating an immutable truth, we open the door to alternative narratives.

As I reflect on my own partnership rejection story from the beginning of this book, I can now see how I chose a disempowering narrative. When told I'd have to wait another year for partnership consideration, I interpreted this as a definitive end rather than a temporary setback. I told myself "I'm not good enough" instead of "I need more development in specific areas". I viewed the delay as a judgement of my worth rather than feedback on my readiness. This interpretation led me to walk away entirely—a decision that closed the door on a possibility that might have eventually materialised.

My regret today isn't about "what could have been" if I'd made partner. Rather, it's about how I interpreted events and reacted in that moment. I allowed a single setback to define my narrative, choosing a story of rejection over one of growth and perseverance. Had I framed this experience differently—perhaps as valuable feedback or an opportunity to strengthen my case—I might have approached the situation with resilience instead of resignation. The true failure wasn't being asked to wait another year; it was choosing a story that gave me no path forward except to leave. This realisation has fundamentally changed how I approach setbacks now, always asking myself: "What other story could I tell about this experience that would empower rather than diminish me?"

This isn't about denial or self-deception. The goal isn't to pretend failures didn't happen or to minimise their impact. This is about utility: the best story is the one that puts us in the optimal frame of mind to learn, grow, and demonstrate resilience. It's the narrative that empowers us to move forward productively while maintaining our commitment to truth and learning.

This approach to choosing empowering narratives might mean:

- acknowledging temporary defeat while maintaining faith in eventual success
- recognising our role in a failure while refusing to let it define our identity

- accepting setbacks while remaining curious about what we can learn from them
- admitting mistakes while demonstrating commitment to growth.

The power of choosing the right story extends beyond individual resilience. As we saw with Howard Schultz at Starbucks, the ability to acknowledge failure while maintaining an empowering narrative about learning and improvement can transform entire organisations.

The story you choose about failure doesn't just interpret your past; it shapes your future. Choose one that empowers you to learn, to grow, and to keep moving forward, no matter what setbacks you encounter along the way.

Key takeaways

- Challenge your belief in a single "truth" about failure by deliberately seeking multiple interpretations of setbacks, asking "What else might this mean?" rather than accepting your first negative conclusion.
- Identify and counter your cognitive biases. Perhaps have a trusted colleague review your assessment of failures, providing perspective that cuts through your self-serving or overly harsh interpretations.
- Replace absolutist language like "always", "never", and "disaster" with specific, temporary framing when discussing setbacks to prevent failures from seeming permanent or all-encompassing.

- Create clear separation between your actions and your identity by using language that describes events ("This approach didn't work") rather than character ("I'm a failure at this").

- Actively practise admitting mistakes and sharing lessons learnt, starting with small acknowledgements to build the confidence that transparency enhances rather than damages your credibility.

Part II

Turn setbacks into stepping stones

On extracting the maximum value from every failure

Now you've recognised how fear influences your actions, the next challenge is transforming how you respond when things don't go as planned. Most people either dwell on failures, allowing them to erode confidence, or quickly move past them, missing crucial insights. Both approaches waste the immense value hidden within every setback.

Learning to see failure as feedback will create a fundamental shift in your growth trajectory. By approaching disappointments with curiosity rather than judgement, you'll extract valuable lessons that accelerate your development. And by focusing your energy on what you can control rather than outcomes beyond your influence, you'll maintain momentum despite inevitable obstacles.

This perspective shift delivers powerful advantages: faster skill development through rapid learning cycles, greater resilience when facing challenges, clearer decision-making under pressure, and the paradoxical discovery that letting go of rigid outcome expectations often leads to better results. Instead of being demoralised by setbacks, you'll begin seeing them as rich sources of information guiding your next steps.

The Failure Advantage

The most successful individuals and organisations don't simply tolerate failure—they systematically mine it for insights that drive their next innovations. By developing this capability, you'll transform what most people view as defeats into the very stepping stones that carry you toward your goals.

3.

Failure is just feedback

"Knowledge of our faults is the gateway to correction."
– Benjamin Disraeli

Look under your kitchen sink or in your garage, and you'll likely find a familiar blue and yellow can with a red top. WD-40 has become such a household staple but few know that its name tells a story of persistence through failure. Those seemingly random letters and numbers reveal its origin: water displacement, fortieth formula. That's right, it took 39 failures before creating the miracle spray that would eventually be used by four out of five American households and many more globally.

In the early 1950s, at a house in San Diego's Hillcrest neighbourhood, Iver Norman Lawson was growing increasingly frustrated. A mechanical engineer by training and an innovator by nature, Lawson had already achieved success as the founder of Airtech and even designed a glider for pioneering aviator Charles Lindbergh. But now, he faced a different challenge. A naval commander had approached him with a pressing problem: ocean salt was corroding vital equipment on navy vessels. Could Lawson develop a solution that would resist water and prevent rust?

Night after night, Lawson mixed chemicals in his makeshift laboratory above his garage. Each failed attempt might have discouraged a lesser inventor, but Lawson saw each unsuccessful formula as data; valuable feedback pointing him toward what didn't work and, by extension, what might. Formula after formula, he refined his approach, adjusting ratios and ingredients based on the results of each test. Finally, on his fortieth attempt, something extraordinary happened. The mixture worked perfectly, creating a stable, effective water displacement formula that would protect metal from rust and corrosion. But this was just the beginning of WD-40's story of embracing feedback for growth.

When the Rocket Chemical Company (WD-40's original name) began marketing the product, something unexpected happened. Customers started reporting novel uses for the spray far beyond its intended purpose of preventing rust on naval equipment. Instead of dismissing these unplanned applications, the company's leadership listened. They collected these stories and began to understand that their product's true value lay not in what they thought it should do, but in what their customers were actually using it for. People discovered WD-40 could remove crayon marks from walls, free stuck zippers, and even clean guitar strings. One customer reported using it to remove a python from the undercarriage of a bus in Asia. Another used it to keep pigeons off balconies. The company embraced these discoveries, eventually documenting over 2,000 uses for their product. Each new application was treated as valuable feedback that shaped their marketing and distribution strategies.

The results speak for themselves. From humble beginnings as a rust preventative for missiles, WD-40 grew into a global phenomenon. By 1993, the company's revenue reached over $100

3. Failure is just feedback

million, and today it sells in more than 176 countries. The formula remains so valuable it's never been patented, instead being kept as a closely guarded trade secret.

For me, the real secret to WD-40's success wasn't in the chemical formula, it was in the company's relationship with failure and feedback. First, Lawson persisted through 39 failed formulas, each one providing crucial data for the next attempt. Then through the company's willingness to listen to unexpected customer feedback and pivot their entire marketing approach based on what they learnt. They understood that failure and feedback weren't obstacles to success—they were the fuel for growth.

This mindset, of treating failure as feedback and feedback as fuel for growth, is far more valuable than any secret formula. It's a mindset that characterises not just successful products, but successful people and organisations. Yet despite its power, it's surprisingly rare. Most of us instinctively resist feedback and avoid failure at all costs, missing countless opportunities for growth and innovation in the process.

In this chapter, we'll explore why feedback is so fundamental to growth, why we often resist it, and how we can learn to embrace it. We'll see how feedback loops are woven into the fabric of nature itself, and how the most successful human enterprises, from scientific discovery to business innovation, rely on systematic feedback for continuous improvement. Most importantly, we'll learn how to transform our relationship with feedback from one of fear to one of opportunity.

Like WD-40's creators, we'll discover that the true formula for success often lies in what we learn from our failures.

Leverage failure for competitive edge

Nature's most fundamental truth is elegantly simple: adapt or fade away. This principle, far from being limited to the natural world, holds profound implications for our personal and professional lives. Yet while we intellectually understand this concept, we often resist one of its most essential components: feedback, particularly when it comes in the form of failure.

For an illustration of this principle at work in nature, then look no further than Galápagos finches which have provided one of science's most compelling demonstrations of adaptation through feedback. For nearly four decades, researchers Peter and Rosemary Grant studied these remarkable birds, meticulously documenting how their very anatomy changed in response to environmental feedback. During one particularly severe drought, only finches with larger beaks survived because they alone could crack open the tough, spiny seeds that remained when other food sources were depleted. Within this single event, the average beak depth of the population increased by one millimetre, a small change that meant the difference between life and death. This dramatic shift in physical characteristics, occurring within a single generation, demonstrates how feedback drives not just survival, but improvement.

The implications for our personal and professional lives are striking. Just as finches must adapt to changing food sources, we must continuously adjust our approaches based on the feedback we receive. A business leader reading market signals, a teacher gauging student engagement, or a software developer analysing user behaviour, all are participating in feedback loops that determine their effectiveness. Success in any domain isn't a static achievement but rather a dynamic process of constant adaptation.

What's just as fascinating is how modern research has shattered our previous assumptions about the pace of adaptation. One example is Professor David Reznick's work with guppies in Trinidad. When these fish were introduced to new environments with different predator pressures, they evolved significant changes in their growth rates and reproductive strategies in just ten years, a blink of an eye in evolutionary terms. This reveals another profound truth: adaptation can happen far more rapidly than we once believed possible.

I think we should reflect on these revelations with respect to our own development. Those individuals and organisations who can respond to feedback rapidly can gain significant advantage. Personally, individuals who take note of feedback they receive, take on learnings, and adjust their approach will get better results over those who fend off criticism. Leaders who actively seek and respond to the views of those around them typically gain more influence and build more effective organisations. In business, companies that can rapidly respond to changing markets and customer feedback usually outperform their slower paced rivals.

But the reason this proves to be an advantage highlights a peculiar phenomenon—not everyone behaves this way. Feedback, particularly negative feedback, is often resisted despite overwhelming evidence that responding to feedback is essential for growth and adaptation. Our instinct is again to resist negative feedback, perhaps even deny its existence in the interests of self-protection or to avoid the need to change.

This resistance becomes even more puzzling when we consider that feedback systems are woven into the very fabric of our existence. From the simplest biological processes to the most complex ecosystems, nature demonstrates that feedback isn't just beneficial; it's essential for survival and growth. So why do we, as conscious beings capable of intentional improvement, often choose to ignore or reject this fundamental tool for advancement?

The answer to this question lies in understanding the psychological barriers that stand between us and effective feedback processing.

We say we want feedback, but we don't

Imagine you're driving a car with a broken dashboard. The fuel gauge doesn't work, the temperature warning light is disconnected, and the speedometer is dark. Most of us would find this situation unbearable or at least dangerous. Yet in our professional and personal lives, we often willingly operate with our feedback sensors turned off, creating blind spots that can lead to equally dangerous outcomes.

This resistance to feedback presents one of the great paradoxes of human behaviour. Our bodies are masterpieces of feedback engineering—maintaining temperature, adjusting hormone levels, and balancing countless other systems through continuous feedback loops. We trust these automatic systems implicitly, never questioning their constant adjustments. But when it comes to conscious feedback about our performance, decisions, or behaviours, we often become remarkably adept at avoidance.

3. Failure is just feedback

The science of cognitive psychology helps us understand this seemingly irrational behaviour. In Chapter 2 I discussed "confirmation bias", a tendency to search for, interpret, and recall information in ways that confirm our existing beliefs while giving disproportionately less consideration to alternative possibilities. With respect to feedback, this natural tendency can blind us to crucial information about our performance and potential areas for improvement. We only pay attention to data that confirms what we already believe.

Even more intriguing is the "ostrich effect", named after the myth that ostriches bury their heads in sand when facing danger. Studies in behavioural economics have shown that individuals are more likely to check their investment portfolios when markets are rising than when they're falling. This same pattern appears in numerous professional contexts: employees avoiding performance reviews after difficult projects, entrepreneurs neglecting to analyse failed initiatives, or managers postponing conversations about team conflicts. The irony is that this avoidance behaviour creates a self-reinforcing cycle. High-performing individuals and organisations share a common trait: they actively seek out negative feedback. Similarly, successful organisations have cultures where feedback, especially critical feedback, is not just accepted but actively solicited. These organisations understand that negative feedback, while temporarily uncomfortable, provides the most direct path to improvement.

In contrast, underperforming organisations often exhibit what psychologists call "organisational defensive routines", patterns of behaviour that protect people from experiencing embarrassment or threat while simultaneously preventing them from identifying and correcting the causes of those potential embarrassments or threats. These routines can become so ingrained that they create a form of institutional blindness, where problems are systematically ignored or rationalised away.

Perhaps most insidious is what I call the "illusion of feedback", where there is a gap between our perceived openness to feedback and our actual behavioural response to it. In surveys, an overwhelming majority of professionals claim they welcome constructive criticism and value honest feedback. Yet behavioural studies tell a different story. When faced with actual negative feedback, many of these same individuals exhibit avoidance behaviours, defensive responses, or what psychologists call "motivated forgetting", selectively remembering positive feedback while discounting or forgetting negative input.

This illusion is particularly damaging because it allows us to maintain a self-image of someone who is open to growth whilst simultaneously protecting us from the discomfort of criticism or the need to change. We delude ourselves—like the fitness enthusiast who wears all the latest brand name kit and looks like they just stepped out of the gym never having actually visited it. The gap between our self-image and our actual behaviours can widen over time so understanding these mental barriers becomes important to self-correction. By recognising these patterns, we can begin to develop strategies to counteract them and can work with our psychology rather than against it.

Apply the scientist's mindset

Having studied business and economics to a post-graduate level, and spent years in practice and in leadership, I had been led to believe that management and personal development was generally based on a sound set of principles and methodologies, refined over the ages, designed to ensure sustained evolution and improvement. But it was only when I was introduced to the scientific method that I realised how immature and imprecise our personal development and management methods are at measuring and responding to feedback. While we often think of it as the domain of researchers in white lab coats, at its core, the scientific method is humanity's most refined feedback system; a systematic way to learn from both success and failure. Its power lies not in complexity, but in its commitment to reality over assumption.

Coming back to the Galápagos finches, the Grants' groundbreaking research wasn't just about observing birds; it was about applying rigorous scientific methodology to understand evolution in action. For 40 years, they meticulously measured beak sizes, tracked individual birds, documented breeding patterns, and recorded environmental conditions. When a severe drought yielded surprising changes in the finch population, they didn't rely on casual observation or gut feeling—they had hard data showing the precise one-millimetre increase in average beak depth; a small but critical difference that meant survival for some and death for others.

This systematic approach to gathering and analysing feedback offers a powerful model for personal and professional growth. Let's break down the key elements of the scientific method and see how they can transform our approach to feedback:

- **Observation and question:** Scientists begin by carefully observing phenomena and forming specific questions. In business, this might mean moving beyond vague concerns like: "Why aren't we meeting our goals?" to specific, measurable questions: "Which customer segments show declining engagement with our new feature?"

- **Hypothesis formation:** Scientists develop testable explanations for what they observe. In professional settings, this means replacing assumptions with clear, testable predictions: "If we reduce response time to customer inquiries by 50%, customer satisfaction scores will increase by at least 15%."
- **Controlled testing:** Scientific experiments isolate variables to understand cause and effect. While perfect control isn't always possible in business, we can still design structured tests. A/B testing in marketing, pilot programmes for new initiatives, or controlled rollouts of new policies all follow this principle.
- **Data collection and analysis:** Scientists collect comprehensive data, not just evidence that supports their hypothesis. This is where many organisations fall short. They trumpet data that confirms their existing beliefs while ignoring or dismissing contradictory information. True data-driven decision-making requires examining all available evidence, especially data that challenges our assumptions.
- **Revision and iteration:** Perhaps most importantly, scientists view results, even negative ones, as valuable feedback that leads to refined hypotheses and better experiments. This iterative approach is what separates genuinely data-driven organisations from those that merely claim the label.

3. Failure is just feedback

Consider the contrast between two approaches to customer feedback:

Company A claims to be data-driven because they conduct annual customer satisfaction surveys. The results are reviewed in a single meeting, broad conclusions are drawn, and the data is filed away until next year. They're collecting data but not using it as a true feedback system.

Company B, however, approaches customer feedback like a scientific experiment. They continuously gather data from multiple sources, test specific hypotheses about customer behaviour, and maintain controlled groups when rolling out changes. They track metrics in real-time and adjust their approach based on actual results rather than assumptions. When initiatives fail, they conduct detailed post-mortems to understand why, treating each failure as valuable data rather than a disappointment to be forgotten.

The power of applying scientific methodology to business feedback is illustrated by companies like Amazon, whose leadership principles explicitly include "Learn and Be Curious" and "Insist on the Highest Standards". Amazon's famous "working backwards" process—starting with the customer and working backwards to the solution—mirrors the scientific method's systematic approach to problem-solving. Google's rapid experimentation culture provides another example. Their famous A/B testing approach to product development, where they might test 41 different shades of blue for a button to determine which performs best, shows how scientific rigour can be applied to even seemingly subjective decisions. They don't rely on expert opinions or gut feelings, they let data from controlled experiments guide their choices.

But perhaps the most powerful aspect of the scientific method as a feedback model is its inherent humility. Scientists understand that every conclusion is provisional, subject to revision based on new evidence. This mindset of maintaining strong convictions while remaining open to new data is crucial for personal and professional growth.

By adopting the scientific method's principles, we can transform feedback from a sporadic, often uncomfortable event into a systematic, ongoing process of learning and improvement. It provides a framework that helps us overcome our natural biases and resistance to negative feedback, replacing them with a structured approach to gathering and using all available information, positive or negative, to drive growth and innovation.

When I realised my mindset was a problem

Sometimes our most profound insights about growth and learning come not from boardrooms or research papers, but from everyday moments that force us to confront our own assumptions. For me, that moment came in my backyard, playing catch with my son.

I had always considered myself "rubbish at ball sports". Throughout my school years, I had perfected an elaborate array of avoidance techniques: standing at the back during team selections, volunteering to referee rather than play, or engineering convenient schedule conflicts. If a ball was meant to be caught, I would drop it; if it needed to be hit, I would miss; if I was supposed to avoid it, I would somehow end up in its path. I had rationalised this as simply part of who I was, attributing it to my upbringing in a family that prioritised swimming over ball sports.

3. Failure is just feedback

But there I was, in our garden, tossing a ball back and forth with my son. As he struggled with catches and throws, I heard myself saying things like: "You just need more practice" and "Don't give up"; encouragements that directly contradicted the very mindset I had adopted in my own childhood. This moment of cognitive dissonance led me to a profound realisation about the nature of learning and growth.

What I was witnessing was the stark contrast between what psychologists call a "fixed mindset" and a "growth mindset". With a fixed mindset, we view our abilities as static traits; things we either have or don't have, like eye colour or height. With a growth mindset, we see our abilities as malleable qualities that can be developed through effort, good strategies, and input from others. The implications of these mindsets extend far beyond catching balls in a backyard. Research by Carol Dweck and others has shown that these fundamental beliefs about the nature of ability profoundly impact how we interpret and respond to feedback. Those with a fixed mindset tend to:

- view feedback as judgement on their inherent abilities
- avoid challenges that might expose their limitations
- give up quickly when facing obstacles
- see effort as fruitless or a sign of inadequacy
- feel threatened by others' success.

In contrast, those with a growth mindset typically:

- see feedback as information about their current strategy
- embrace challenges as opportunities to learn

- persist in the face of setbacks
- view effort as the path to mastery
- find inspiration in others' success.

The power of mindset is particularly evident in sports and child development. Consider the contrasting approaches of two young athletes receiving similar feedback about their performance. The athlete with a fixed mindset might hear "you need to work on your technique" as a judgement of their natural ability and become discouraged. The athlete with a growth mindset would interpret the same feedback as a roadmap for improvement.

Organisations are increasingly recognising the crucial role of mindset in their culture and performance. Microsoft's transformation under Satya Nadella provides a compelling example. The company shifted from a "know-it-all" culture to a "learn-it-all" culture, embracing what Nadella calls a "growth mindset at scale". This shift wasn't just philosophical; it fundamentally changed how the organisation approached feedback, failure, and innovation. Microsoft began celebrating "failure stories" in company meetings, recognising that each setback provided valuable data for future success. As an employee myself I can attest to the way in which learning has been ingrained in the way the company works from nature of performance reviews to the way software defects are captured and addressed.

Perhaps most powerfully, a growth mindset transforms our relationship with failure itself. Instead of seeing failure as evidence of our limitations, we begin to view it as a rich source of data about what works and what doesn't. Every missed catch, failed project, or unsuccessful initiative becomes not a judgement of our worth

3. Failure is just feedback

but a piece of feedback guiding us toward improvement. This shift in perspective doesn't happen overnight. Like my journey from avoiding balls to teaching ball skills, it often requires us to confront deep-seated beliefs about our capabilities. But the reward is worth the effort; when we truly embrace a growth mindset, we transform feedback from something to be feared into something to be sought out and valued.

The irony of my ball sports story isn't lost on me. By accepting my "inability" as fixed, I had potentially cut myself off from an entire world of experiences and connections. But more importantly, I had embraced a mindset that could have limited me in countless other areas of life. Watching my son learn to catch and throw, I'm reminded that the real challenge isn't developing any particular skill. It's developing the mindset that makes all skill development possible.

The real test is what you do with feedback

It is one thing to understand the importance of feedback, and diligently collect the data, but the real test is whether you actually use it to make changes. This is true for individuals and organisations. Companies often showcase their elaborate feedback systems—customer satisfaction surveys, employee engagement polls, 360-degree reviews—yet many of these impressive-looking mechanisms produce little meaningful change. It's as if we believe the mere act of collecting feedback is enough to drive improvement.

Let me share a revealing experience that exposed this illusion to me. As the head of a customer service function, I oversaw what appeared to be a robust feedback system. We had carefully designed surveys deployed at key points in the customer journey, generating qualitative summaries, verbatim comments, and specific issues for process owners and team leaders. Every month, I received a high-level summary of the results; a dashboard of customer sentiment that supposedly drove our continuous improvement efforts.

Then something unexpected happened. An unrelated system change inadvertently stopped our surveys from being distributed. The truly revealing part? Nobody noticed. Not the process owners who were supposed to be acting on the feedback. Not the team leaders who should have been addressing specific concerns. Not even me. I had missed the absence of the previous month's summary entirely. Two months of silence from our customers, and not a single person had raised an alarm. This moment of realisation was both humbling and instructive. We had created an elaborate feedback theatre; a performance of continuous improvement without the improvement! Our culture had evolved to value the appearance of acting on feedback more than the reality of making changes based on it.

This scenario plays out in organisations worldwide. Companies invest heavily in feedback systems that generate mountains of data but produce no change.

The solution lies in moving beyond simple feedback collection to what organisational theorist Chris Argyris calls "double-loop learning". Traditional single-loop learning asks: "How can we do this better?" Double-loop learning asks: "Why are we doing this at all, and are our fundamental assumptions correct?" With respect to failure, this creates an important shift by opening us to the potential that things may not be successful. By simply asking the question, we are inviting the possibility that our initial position is wrong and removing some of the shock or resistance if the question has an unexpected answer. This, in turn, turns the failure into a data point rather than an identity crisis.

As with all new things, it is best to set up a process or system to get reliable results rather than relying on discipline and willpower alone. Companies that embrace double-loop learning, for example, typically follow a framework for transformation feedback into action:

1. **Feedback collection with purpose:** Before collecting any feedback, they clearly define how it will be used and identify specific decision-makers who will act on the feedback. This creates accountability for acting on insights which also drives timelines.
2. **Analysis that drives action:** They move beyond simple metrics to understand root cause, looking for patterns across different feedback sources, questioning underlying assumptions about what the feedback means.
3. **Implementation planning:** They create clear ownership for each improvement initiative and measurable goals for change including timelines for implementation.
4. **Feedback loop closure:** They communicate actions taken back to feedback providers.

To make this framework effective, you need to develop what I call "action habits"—regular practices that move feedback from insight to implementation. Here are some that have worked well for me personally:

- **Journalling:** Maintaining a simple journal helps me capture events from the day or week and extract the feedback within them. Including a specific prompt, such as "what feedback did I receive today?", directs attention to available learning opportunities. The act of writing not only creates commitment but provides a record to track patterns over time.

- **Feedback conversations:** While we often feel eager to provide others with feedback, how frequently do we seek it ourselves? Each week, I make a point of inviting specific feedback from someone I've interacted with—not with a vague "can you give me feedback?" but with focused questions like "how effective was that meeting I organised on Tuesday?" This approach often yields surprising insights. An additional benefit: regularly reaching out this way signals your openness to feedback, making others more comfortable offering their observations voluntarily.

- **Data tracking:** For every objective you have, personally or professionally, actively identify measurable data points that indicate your progress. A personal goal like "eat healthier" needs concrete indicators that provide feedback—perhaps tracking alcohol consumption or body measurements. Similarly, professional objectives, such as "improve customer service", need to be linked to measures that you can track frequently. This habit of seeking relevant data establishes a continuous feedback loop and, as we'll explore later, helps recognise progress—crucial for sustaining improvement.

By embedding these habits into your routine, you ensure that data, including failure, is consistently identified and acted upon. This creates a more productive relationship with failure. By normalising the identification of failure through a structured process, I've found I can create separation between the failure and myself—it becomes something I'm analysing, not something that defines me. And I've discovered that changing my own approach has transformed not only my outlook but also the culture of my team.

The transformative power of feedback

Let's return to where we began: with a simple can of WD-40 sitting on a shelf in millions of homes worldwide. What appeared at first glance to be merely an interesting piece of trivia, that the name represents the fortieth attempt at creating a "water displacement" formula, now reveals itself as a master class in the principles of effective feedback systems. Consider what it means to fail 39 times in the pursuit of a solution. Each failure could have been interpreted as evidence that the goal was unattainable, that the team lacked the necessary skills, or that the entire project should be abandoned. Instead, the Rocket Chemical Company, and Iver Lawson, exemplified every aspect of effective feedback utilisation we've explored in this chapter.

First, Iver Lawson demonstrated the growth mindset we discussed, viewing each failed attempt not as a dead end but as a data point guiding them toward the goal. He understood intuitively what we now know scientifically—that capability isn't fixed, and that progress comes through persistent, intelligent effort.

His approach mirrored the scientific method we examined. Each iteration wasn't a random modification but part of a systematic process of experimentation and refinement. He collected data, analysed results, adjusted the formula, and tried again. This methodical approach to failure—treating each attempt as a controlled experiment—transformed what could have been merely trial and error into structured learning.

Most importantly, he embodied the principle that feedback without action is meaningless as each failure led to specific changes in their formula. He didn't just observe that attempt number 27 didn't work; he used that information to inform attempt number 28. This action-oriented approach to feedback was crucial to their eventual success. The WD-40 story also illustrates how overcoming our psychological barriers to feedback can lead to extraordinary results. Imagine if he had succumbed to the feedback blind spot we discussed, interpreting early failures as evidence he should abandon the project.

This is the ultimate lesson of feedback: when properly embraced and systematically acted upon, it becomes not just a tool for improvement but a crucial differentiator in both personal and organisational success. In a world where change is constant and competition is fierce, the ability to learn and adapt through effective feedback systems isn't just helpful; it's essential for survival and success.

Key takeaways

- Treat failure as valuable feedback rather than defeat by responding to setbacks with curiosity ("What can I learn from this?") instead of judgement ("Why did I mess up?").
- Apply the scientific method to your approach by formulating clear hypotheses before acting, then objectively analysing both successes and failures for meaningful patterns.

- Overcome feedback resistance by creating structured systems that require you to review results objectively, preventing avoidance of uncomfortable information.
- Cultivate a growth mindset by replacing fixed statements ("I'm not good at this") with process-oriented language ("I haven't mastered this yet") to keep your focus on improvement rather than judgement.
- Establish regular "action reviews" where you translate insights from failures into specific changes to your approach, ensuring feedback becomes transformation rather than just information.

4.

Focus on what you can control

"The more you fixate on the finish line, the more likely you are to trip over your own feet."

Growing up in Australia and living much of my life in Sydney I never spared much thought for the Sydney Opera House. It was just always there and would certainly be in the scene if I was asked to conjure "Sydney" in my mind, more of a symbol than as a working building. In some ways it is Sydney to me. It was only after having travelled and explored more of the world that I realised how groundbreaking and unique was the design. And only recently did I learn that at one point in 1966, the Sydney Opera House was considered a catastrophic failure. It was little more than a hole in the ground, its budget had ballooned from the initial estimate of $7 million to over $20 million, and it was years behind schedule. Yet today, it stands as one of the most celebrated buildings in human history, a UNESCO World Heritage site visited by millions, and an enduring symbol of human creativity and ambition.

What happened? And why does this matter to our relationship with failure? I think the story of the Sydney Opera House perfectly illustrates a fundamental problem that plagues our lives: our obsession with predetermined outcomes blinds us to the very process required to achieve greatness. We fixate on the destination—the perfect building, the quarterly target, the career milestone—while ignoring the uncertain, messy journey required to get there.

From its inception, the Opera House carried immense expectations. Premier Joseph Cahill set very specific outcomes: a budget of $7 million and completion by 26 January 1963. But this outcome fixation contained a fatal flaw and set the project up for failure—the pressure to commit to specific timelines and budgets before the building's revolutionary design challenges were fully understood. The estimates were based on conventional construction methods, but Jørn Utzon's design was anything but conventional. The now-iconic shell-shaped roof posed engineering challenges that would take years to solve. Even the geology of the site had been misunderstood. Yet rather than revise expectations based on these discoveries, political pressure to deliver the original promised outcomes mounted.

By 1966, three years after the planned completion date, Utzon himself walked away from his career-defining project. The very outcomes that forced him from the project, increased costs and extended timelines, were inevitable given the building's unprecedented nature. The obsession with meeting original estimates, damaged careers, strained relationships, and nearly derailed one of architecture's greatest achievements.

This pattern repeats itself daily in businesses and careers everywhere. We become so attached to specific outcomes that are rarely in our complete control—revenue targets, project deadlines, career milestones—that we lose sight of what actually creates those outcomes: the process, the learning, and most importantly, the elements within our control. There are usually many factors that

4. Focus on what you can control

determine the eventual outcome and focusing solely on the end goal, or factors that can't be influenced, can distract us from what we can actually do.

The breakthrough that ultimately allowed the Opera House to be completed came when attention shifted from predetermined outcomes to the fundamental problem itself. After years of experimentation, Utzon discovered that all the shells could be derived from sections of a single sphere—the "spherical solution". This elegant answer emerged not from fixating on budgets and schedules, but from deep engagement with the work itself.

The final cost was $102 million, and it took 14 years rather than four to complete. But these budget overruns and missed deadlines—the very metrics by which it was once judged a failure—have faded into historical footnotes. What endures is the building itself, rising from Sydney Harbour as proof that our greatest achievements often come not from rigid adherence to predetermined outcomes, but from allowing the process to reveal the path forward.

This tension between outcome-fixation and process-orientation plays out not just in monumental architecture, but in our businesses, careers, and personal projects every day. When we become overly attached to specific outcomes, we risk missing opportunities, stifling innovation, and creating unnecessary pressure that paradoxically makes those outcomes harder to achieve. Our relationship with failure transforms when we shift focus from outcomes we can't fully control to the process that is within our influence. The alternative—focusing on what we can control while maintaining flexible goals—offers a more sustainable and ultimately more successful approach to achievement.

The Failure Advantage

The plan is always wrong

Modern business operates on a fundamental logical flaw: to secure resources for future success, companies must first convince others they can predict that future with certainty. A startup seeking venture capital funding must present detailed financial projections showing exactly how much revenue they'll generate and when they'll become profitable. An established company must provide earnings guidance to Wall Street, committing to specific growth targets quarters or years in advance. Even internal operations revolve around this pretence of predictability—annual budgets, quarterly targets, and project timelines all rest on the assumption that we can accurately forecast outcomes. Not even the best business leaders can tell the future.

This system isn't arbitrary. Investors, whether venture capitalists or public shareholders, need some basis for valuing their investments. Boards need ways to evaluate management performance. Employees need goals to work toward. The entire machinery of modern business depends on our ability to make and fulfil promises about future results. Companies that most consistently hit their targets are rewarded with higher valuations, lower costs of capital, and greater operational flexibility. This creates immense pressure to not only predict the future but to then bend reality to match those predictions.

Yet this pressure collides with a fundamental quirk of human psychology known as the "planning fallacy". First identified by Nobel laureate Daniel Kahneman and Amos Tversky in 1979, the planning fallacy reveals our persistent tendency to underestimate how long tasks will take and how much they will cost, even when we have extensive experience with similar projects running over time and budget. This isn't mere optimism bias—it's a systematic error in how we process information when planning.

Like the Sydney Opera House, our estimates are consistently wrong. And not just by a little, but by orders of magnitude. Infrastructure projects provide an archive of failures with easy-to-understand measures. One infamous example is Boston's "Big Dig" highway project which, when proposed in 1982, was estimated to cost $2.8 billion and be completed by 1998. The final cost? It came in at $22 billion, with completion in 2007! What's remarkable isn't just the magnitude of the miscalculation, but how common such miscalculations are. In the book *How Big Things Get Done* authors Bent Flyvbjerg and Dan Gardner draw on data collated from 16,000 projects from 20 different fields to find that less than 1% are completed on time or budget. And although the mean cost overrun is 62% the distribution has a "fat tail" indicating some true mega fails.

The planning fallacy operates through several mechanisms. First, we tend to focus on the ideal scenario—what psychologists call the "inside view"—rather than looking at how similar projects have actually played out (the "outside view"). Second, we break complex projects into component parts and estimate each piece individually, failing to account for how problems in one area cascade through the entire system. Third, we discount the role of unknown unknowns; those challenges we couldn't possibly anticipate because we've never encountered them before.

Perhaps the most interesting thing about the planning fallacy is what it reveals about human nature: that we like to think that we can control outcomes and failure. We'll ignore mountains of historic evidence to maintain an illusion of control and predictability. It's why executives continue to provide precise earnings guidance when many studies show the guidance to rarely be so accurate, and why project managers continue to develop five-year plans despite knowing that assumptions will change many times before that point is reached. Unfortunately, the cost of this self-deception goes beyond missed deadlines and budget overruns. When we stake our credibility on hitting specific targets, we often resort to damaging behaviours to achieve them, sometimes at the cost of the very outcome we were supposed to be seeking. Long-term targets may be sacrificed for short-term milestones, innovation may be lost due to the need to for predictable results, shortcuts in quality and substance may be pursued to provide the illusion of progress. The underlying pressure to deliver predetermined outcomes can subtly shape everything we do, and usually not for the better.

I'm not suggesting that planning is futile and should be abandoned, or that we shouldn't set goals, either as individuals or as organisations. Only that we should perhaps hold the target more loosely—as an ambition and direction—rather than an inevitability of a detailed plan. Instead of pretending that we can control the outcome, we need to acknowledge the basic truth that the future is uncertain and cannot be known or fully controlled. What if we shifted our focus from hitting specific targets to focusing on robust processes that respond to changing circumstances? What if we measured our success not by how close we stuck to the original plan but how we adapted to inevitable surprises, and carried on toward the ultimate goal anyway?

Such questions point toward a different way of operating—one that treats the future not as something to be predicted and controlled, but as something to be actively shaped through intelligent trial and error.

Admit the outcome is out of your control

Having acknowledged that the plan is likely flawed, the next thing to realise is that you don't have control over every element required to achieve it anyway. In the year 65 ce, a messenger rushed to inform the Roman philosopher Seneca that Emperor Nero had sentenced him to death. The news, while grave, did not seem to disturb the elderly Stoic's composure. He calmly gathered his family, advised them to find strength in remembering his teachings rather than dwelling in grief, and proceeded to carry out the emperor's orders with dignified acceptance. In his final moments, Seneca demonstrated one of the core principles of Stoic philosophy: the critical distinction between what we can and cannot control.

This ancient wisdom carries profound implications for modern achievement. The Stoics understood that conflating what is within our control with what lies beyond it leads not just to unnecessary suffering, but to compromised performance. As Epictetus, another prominent Stoic philosopher, wrote: "The chief task in life is simply this: to identify and separate matters so that I can say clearly to myself which are externals not under my control, and which have to do with the choices I actually control."

To use a more modern example, consider a sales professional preparing for a crucial pitch meeting.

Outside their control:

- whether the client is in a good mood
- if a competitor has already won the deal through back channels
- whether the client's budget gets unexpectedly cut
- if the decision-maker gets replaced mid-process.

Within their control:

- how thoroughly they research the client's needs
- the clarity and persuasiveness of their presentation
- their level of preparation for potential questions
- how they conduct themselves during the meeting
- their follow-up communication strategy.

The mental benefits of this distinction are striking. Focusing on what we can control reduces anxiety, increases resilience, and improves decision-making under pressure. When we stop expending mental and emotional energy on outcomes beyond our influence, we free up those resources for the actions that actually matter, and the outcome is likely better. A salesperson fixated on the outcome, like winning the deal at all costs, might resort to desperate tactics if the meeting starts going poorly, undermining their professional credibility. In contrast, one focused on executing what they can control is more likely to maintain composure and actually perform better, ironically improving their chances of success.

Importantly, accepting the limits of control doesn't mean adopting a passive stance toward achievement. Rather, it means

4. Focus on what you can control

directing our energy more effectively and remaining open to opportunities we couldn't have predicted. This openness to emergence—letting go of rigid predetermined outcomes while maintaining clear direction—characterises many of history's greatest achievements. Alexander Fleming didn't set out to discover penicillin; he was attentive enough to notice and investigate an unexpected pattern in his petri dishes. The Post-it note emerged from a failed attempt to create a super-strong adhesive. In each case, success came not from controlling outcomes but from skilfully engaging with the process.

The paradox is that by releasing our grip on outcomes, we often become more likely to achieve them. When we stop trying to force results that are beyond our control, we become more attuned to actual possibilities. We make better decisions because we're responding to reality rather than our preconceptions about how things "should" be. We spot opportunities we might have missed if we were too focused on our original goal.

The best organisations focus on what they can control

The shift from outcome obsession to what you can control requires a fundamental reorientation toward focusing on inputs rather than outputs. While results matter, they are ultimately the product of countless individual actions and decisions that lie within our sphere of influence. Understanding and mastering these controllable factors creates the foundation for sustainable success.

Consider the basic elements that any business can control, regardless of market conditions or competitive dynamics. Process design and optimisation, quality standards and controls, employee training and development, operational systems and workflows, customer service protocols, and internal communication frameworks all fall squarely within an organisation's power to shape and improve. These "controllables" might seem mundane compared to grand strategic visions or ambitious growth targets, but they often hold the key to lasting competitive advantage.

The concept of core competencies, first introduced by C. K. Prahalad and Gary Hamel, provides a powerful framework for understanding how mastery of controllable inputs can translate into market leadership. Core competencies are the fundamental strengths or strategic capabilities that distinguish a company from its competitors. They're built through sustained investment in and focus on specific controllable aspects of the business—and once developed, they can be leveraged across multiple markets and products.

Amazon offers a lesson in how relentless focus on controllable inputs can evolve into transformative competitive advantages. In its early days, Amazon obsessed over three elements entirely within its control: operational efficiency, customer experience, and technological infrastructure. The company invested heavily in warehouse automation, developed sophisticated inventory management systems, and built robust cloud computing capabilities to support its operations. These weren't glamorous initiatives, but they were areas where focused effort could yield measurable improvements. What began as internal process optimisation eventually grew into entirely new business opportunities. Amazon Web Services (AWS), now a leading cloud computing platform, emerged from the company's efforts to perfect its own IT infrastructure. The company's mastery of logistics and fulfilment operations became the foundation for its third-party marketplace and

4. Focus on what you can control

fulfilment services. By focusing on controllable inputs rather than just sales targets or market share goals, Amazon built capabilities that opened up entirely new horizons for growth.

The same principles apply on an individual level in professional development. When we examine the most successful careers across industries, a pattern emerges: sustained achievement comes not from chasing specific positions or titles, but from methodical development of controllable professional capabilities. These controllable factors fall into several key categories, each offering rich opportunities for focused improvement.

Technical excellence

The foundation of professional value lies in the mastery of your craft, whatever it may be. For an accountant, this might mean knowing tax codes and developing deep expertise in financial analysis and reporting systems. For a designer, it may extend beyond software proficiency to understanding principles of user psychology and behaviour. The key is approaching technical skills not as a checklist to be completed but as a practice to be continuously refined. This might mean dedicating time each week to learning new techniques, experimenting with different approaches, or studying advances in your field.

Communication mastery

Perhaps no controllable factor has a greater impact on career trajectory than communication ability. This encompasses written communication—from emails to presentations to technical documentation—as well as verbal and interpersonal skills. The beauty of communication as a focus area is that every workday provides countless opportunities for deliberate practice. You can refine how you structure your messages, experiment with different approaches to difficult conversations, or work on making complex information more accessible to diverse audiences.

Relationship building

While you can't control how others respond to you, you can control your approach to professional relationships. This includes how you support colleagues, how you participate in meetings, how you handle conflicts, and how you contribute to team culture. Systematic investment in relationship building might involve practices like regular check-ins with team members, actively seeking ways to help others succeed, or building bridges across organisational silos.

Work quality standards

The standards you set for your own work are entirely within your control. This includes attention to detail, thoroughness of analysis, rigorous testing of ideas, and commitment to excellence in execution. High personal quality standards, consistently applied, become a professional signature that distinguishes your work and builds trust with colleagues and clients alike.

Learning

In a business environment that seems to change faster by every passing week, your ability to learn becomes a critical controllable factor. This includes whether you seek out new information, how you process feedback, whether you remain curious to change, and whether you learn from your mistakes. Developing strong learning habits, such as daily reading, deliberate networking, taking formal courses or being mentored, are all controllable activities that can create sustained competitive advantage.

Personal organisation

The most powerful resource you can control is your attention and this comes through personal organisation. How you allocate your time, manage your priorities, and spend your energy impacts everything you do and how it gets done. Basic habits, such as tracking commitments, managing expectations, sorting the important from the unimportant, and being deliberate about what gets your attention, have a massive impact on your effectiveness. I have noticed that these topics often receive focus early in our lives or careers, when we're first experiencing independence from a pre-structured upbringing, for example, but then that focus disappears as we move on in life. The assumption may be that we have mastered these practices, but the irony is we need to hone our personal organisation even more as life progresses and competing demands for our time and attention grow.

The power of focusing on these controllable factors lies in their compounding nature. Small, consistent investments in any of these areas tend to yield exponential returns over time. A modest improvement in communication skill might lead to better project outcomes, which creates opportunities for larger responsibilities, which in turn provides platforms for further skill development. By focusing on these controllable inputs rather than specific career outcomes, you often achieve better outcomes than if you had pursued them directly. A worker who focuses on becoming genuinely excellent at their craft, building strong relationships, and consistently delivering high-quality work is more likely to be promoted than one who simply focuses on getting promoted as the goal. The former builds real capability, the latter might achieve the title without developing the underlying competencies needed for success in the role.

You'll find satisfaction in mastery

At an individual level this change in focus not only offers better results but also provides the opportunity to reduce anxiety as our fixation on outcomes creates a peculiar form of mental torture. We stake our sense of success on results we can't fully control, then wonder why we feel anxious and inadequate. When these arbitrary benchmarks become our definition of success, we set ourselves up for perceived failure even when we're doing good work. The alternative isn't to abandon ambition or stop pursuing challenging goals. Rather, it's to redirect our focus toward what is known as "mastery orientation"—the pursuit of excellence through continuous improvement and deep engagement with the work itself. This shift in focus provides a powerful antidote to outcome obsession and its attendant fears.

The research on mastery orientation reveals fascinating insights about human motivation and performance. Carol Dweck's studies show that individuals with a mastery orientation demonstrate greater resilience, higher creativity, and more sustained motivation over time. But the benefits go deeper. Research by Edward Deci and Richard Ryan on Self-Determination Theory has found that mastery experiences fulfil our fundamental psychological need for competence, leading to what they call "autonomous motivation"—a form of motivation that can sustain effort and engagement far longer than external rewards or pressures.

This finding has important implications for long-term achievement and personal growth. While outcome-focused motivation tends to diminish once a goal is reached (or missed), mastery-oriented motivation can actually increase with time and challenge.

4. Focus on what you can control

Studies of expert performers across fields, from musicians to athletes to chess players, show that those who maintain high levels of practice and performance over decades typically focus on mastery rather than achievement. They experience what psychologists call "flow states" more frequently, those optimal experiences where challenge and skill align to create deep engagement and satisfaction.

Consider the contrasting approaches of two software development teams. Team A focuses exclusively on hitting delivery deadlines and feature counts. They take shortcuts to meet arbitrary targets, accumulate technical debt, and become increasingly stressed as quality issues mount. Team B, while still mindful of deadlines, prioritises writing clean, well-tested code and improving their development practices. They might occasionally deliver more slowly, but their code is more reliable, their system more maintainable, and their team more capable over time.

The pursuit of mastery shares common elements, even though their application may look very different when applied in specific fields:

1. Focus on fundamentals

It is said that when legendary basketball coach John Wooden started each season at UCLA, he began by teaching his players how to properly put on their socks and tie their shoes. This wasn't eccentricity—it was a deliberate emphasis on mastering fundamentals that would prevent blisters and injuries. His teams went on to win 10 NCAA championships in 12 years. Back to our Amazon example, their early success came not from flashy innovations but from relentless refinement of basic e-commerce operations: faster page loads, better search, more efficient fulfilment.

2. Embrace of feedback

Pixar's success in producing consistent hits stems not from chasing market trends but from their rigorous story development process. Every film goes through multiple complete revisions, with regular feedback from their "brain trust" of experienced storytellers. The focus isn't on making sure each film succeeds commercially, but on making each film as good as it can possibly be.

3. Investment in learning

When hedge fund manager Ray Dalio started Bridgewater Associates, he began documenting every significant decision and its outcome, creating a system of "principles" that could be tested and refined over time. This systematic approach to learning helped Bridgewater become the world's largest hedge fund, but more importantly, it created a culture of intellectual growth and continuous improvement.

4. Attention to process

Chef Thomas Keller, whose restaurants have earned multiple Michelin stars, is famous for his attention to minute details—how vegetables are cut, how dishes are plated, how kitchens are organised. This focus on process excellence, rather than just final results, has created some of the world's most celebrated dining experiences.

The power of mastery orientation comes from its alignment with how our brains are wired for learning and satisfaction. According to some research, the pursuit of mastery activates our reward systems differently than the pursuit of external outcomes. While achieving a goal provides a short satisfaction spike, the engaged pursuit of mastery triggers a sustained release of chemicals associated with wellbeing and satisfaction. This creates a sustainable cycle of motivation that can fuel decades of dedicated practice and improvement.

This sustained engagement is what enables extraordinary achievements. Anders Ericsson's research on expert performance shows that the key difference between good performers and great ones isn't talent but rather the ability to maintain deliberate practice over long periods. Mastery orientation makes this possible by providing intrinsic rewards that don't depend on external outcomes.

The power of mastery orientation extends beyond individual achievement to organisational culture. Companies that foster mastery-oriented environments typically see:

- higher employee engagement and retention
- more innovation and creative problem-solving
- better quality outputs and customer satisfaction
- greater resilience during market downturns
- stronger long-term performance.

This isn't to suggest that outcomes don't matter—they do. But by focusing on mastery rather than specific results, we create the conditions that make positive outcomes more likely while building capabilities that serve us regardless of any particular outcome. A sales team focused on mastering customer understanding will likely hit their quotas more consistently than one focused solely on numbers. A product team devoted to deeply understanding user needs will likely create more successful products than one chasing competitor features.

The shift from outcome obsession to mastery orientation requires both individual and organisational change. It means redefining success metrics to include process quality and capability development, not just results. It means creating environments where experimentation and learning are valued alongside achievement. Most importantly, it means finding intrinsic motivation in the work itself rather than just its external rewards.

Have goals, but treat them as a compass

The shift from outcome obsession to mastery shouldn't be misinterpreted as complete abandonment of goals and targets. Rather, it represents a more sophisticated approach to achievement—one that recognises both the necessity of direction and the importance of flexibility in how we get there. Like a compass on a journey, outcomes provide essential orientation while leaving room for discovering better paths along the way.

There is no avoiding the reality that modern business operates on measurable results; quarterly targets, annual budgets, and strategic goals serve vital functions in coordinating collective effort and allocating resources effectively. Investors need returns, employees need salaries, and customers need reliable products and services, so simply declaring freedom from all metrics and targets is impractical and would put you in opposition with the world. The key lies in how we relate to these necessary measures of progress. There is a difference between treating outcomes as inevitabilities versus viewing them as possibilities. When we see targets as absolute requirements that must be achieved in exactly the way we've envisioned, we create a mental cage and can restrict our ability to find innovative solutions. But when we hold these same targets as ambitious goals, important destinations we're working toward while remaining open to different routes, we maintain both direction and creative freedom.

The same opportunity is available with respect to personal and professional goals. Having a clear career aspiration is valuable; it helps filter opportunities and guide development choices. But treating that aspiration as a fixed destination that must be reached through a predetermined path often leads to missed opportunities and unnecessary stress. Holding the goal lightly while focusing intensely on developing relevant capabilities will likely create more space for serendipity and alternative paths to success. Practically speaking, this balance might look like:

- maintaining clear and ambitious goals, but remaining flexible about how you will achieve them
- regularly reviewing whether current activities and focus align with desired outcomes (outcomes, not pre-planned tasks)
- willingness to adjust both strategies and targets as new information emerges
- measuring and valuing process improvements alongside outcome metrics
- deliberate experimentation and learning.

The art lies in holding outcomes firmly enough to provide direction, but loosely enough to allow for emergence and adaptation. This is not always comfortable, as it requires tolerating ambiguity and maintaining faith that solid process will eventually yield desired results, but this balanced approach ultimately creates better conditions for both individual and organisational success.

As we navigate the complexities of modern business and career development, the ability to maintain this dynamic balance becomes increasingly valuable. Markets change, technologies evolve, and opportunities emerge in unexpected places. Those who can hold clear direction while remaining adaptive in their approach—who can focus on controllable inputs while staying aligned with desired outcomes—are best positioned to thrive in this environment.

Let go of the outcome and you might even achieve it

The greatest irony of outcome obsession is that it often prevents the very achievements we seek. Like athletes who fumble due to their fixation on the finish line, our obsession on future outcomes can freeze us in the present moment, making failure more likely rather than less.

Not only can we improve outcomes through focusing on inputs but there is also profound liberation in redirecting our attention to what lies before us right now: the next step, the current challenge, the immediate opportunity for improvement, what we can control. When we release our death grip on predetermined outcomes and instead embrace the practice of mastery, we don't just reduce our fear of failure; we fundamentally redefine our relationship with it. Each setback becomes data rather than disaster. Each mistake becomes an opportunity rather than a judgement.

And this shift can do more than just ease our anxiety; it can unleash our potential. When we are free from the mental burden of guaranteeing outcomes, we become more creative, more resilient, and more effective. We'll likely take smarter risks because we're no longer paralysed by the prospect of failure and our decisions will be better because we're responding to reality rather than clinging to preconceptions.

So, the path to extraordinary results, it turns out, lies not in more rigid control but in conscious release. Release of the illusion that we can perfectly predict and control outcomes, of the need to know exactly how our efforts will unfold. And release of the fear that anything less than perfect execution equals failure. In this release, we find clarity rather than chaos and higher performance rather than lower standards.

My advice: shift more of your focus from the unpredictable future to the actual present. Pour your energy into mastering what you can control rather than worrying about what you can't. Find satisfaction in the quality of your effort rather than just the results. And trust that by doing so you're not abandoning your ambitions but creating the best conditions for their achievement.

Key takeaways

- The modern world forces us to focus on outcomes, but these are rarely within our control. Recognise the planning fallacy and acknowledge that our predictions are systematically optimistic regardless of experience.

- Identify what's truly within your control and separate the factors you can directly influence and external variables that you can't control. Redirect your energy exclusively to the former.

- Develop mastery in controllable professional capabilities, like technical excellence, communication skill, and work quality standards, rather than fixating on outcomes, like promotions or recognition.
- Reframe goals as directional guidance rather than rigid requirements, allowing yourself to adapt to changing circumstances while maintaining your overall purpose.
- Practise detachment from outcomes by focusing on thorough preparation and excellent execution while mentally releasing attachment to specific results, paradoxically improving your chances of success.

Part III

Progress over perfection

On building momentum through consistent imperfect action

Knowledge without action has little value. Even with a healthier perspective on failure, many of us remain stuck in planning and preparation—waiting for the perfect moment, the perfect plan, or the perfect skill level—before taking meaningful action.

The shift from preparation to progress happens when you embrace imperfect action and small wins. Starting before you feel fully ready breaks the paralysis of perfectionism and generates real-world feedback that no amount of planning can provide. Building systems for consistent small steps creates unstoppable momentum that transforms seemingly impossible goals into inevitable achievements.

This action-oriented approach delivers results: projects that actually launch rather than remaining perpetually "almost ready", rapid improvement cycles that outpace competitors who wait for perfection, reduced anxiety as progress replaces pressure, and the motivational power of visible momentum that fuels continued effort.

The most productive people aren't those with superhuman discipline or flawless execution—they're those who consistently take

The Failure Advantage

imperfect action and maintain forward progress despite obstacles. By adopting these practical strategies for sustained momentum, you'll bridge the gap between knowing what to do and actually doing it, turning potential into tangible outcomes.

5.

Start before you're ready

"The man who makes no mistakes does not usually make anything." – Edward John Phelps

An inconvenient truth is behind every delayed project, every unopened business, every unwritten book, and every dream deferred. Someone was waiting for the ideal moment, when the right conditions prevailed, or for the perfect plan, but it never arrived. The pursuit of perfection paralyses progress, and it's a trap that rather than delivering excellence, usually results in nothing. In reality, we're often hiding behind perfection to avoid the very actions necessary to bring our dreams to life. But taking action, however imperfect, is the most important step toward achieving your goals and building the momentum required for eventual success. This isn't just motivational self-help; it's a principle proven many times over by those who have achieved great things and moved past many setbacks.

This realisation came to me when I heard Reid Hoffman, the founder of LinkedIn, telling the story of how the platform started. I was surprised to learn that when he launched the platform in 2003 it was a long way short of his aspiration. The interface looked nothing like his vision, there were no profile photos, users couldn't send attachments, and other basic features anyone would consider critical were missing. Every instinct screamed to wait, to add the next feature, to streamline the experience, to test a little more—the voice of perfectionism was saying "not good enough" and providing the perfect excuse to delay.

But he launched anyway.

The initial version of LinkedIn was so basic that Hoffman felt the need to add "early adopter" to every profile—a subtle apology for the platform's limitations. In his mind, it wasn't just imperfect; it was embarrassing. Yet this "embarrassing" version of LinkedIn, launched before it was complete, before it was polished, and long before Hoffman felt fully ready, became the foundation of what would grow into a platform worth over $30 billion, connecting more than 900 million professionals worldwide.

Reflecting on that launch, Hoffman recounts discovering something surprising: that many of the features he thought essential weren't necessary, and user feedback resulted in the development of other features that he hadn't envisioned. In launching early, he had saved months or years of unnecessary effort and accelerated the development of features that were actually needed. This experience led him to coin what would become a guiding principle for Silicon Valley entrepreneurs: "If you're not embarrassed by your first product release, you've launched too late."

This philosophy challenges everything we've been taught about excellence and achievement. From childhood, we're conditioned to believe that anything worth doing is worth doing perfectly. We're praised for flawless test scores, perfect attendance, and immaculate presentations. This conditioning creates a dangerous illusion; that success requires perfection, and that imperfect action is worse than no action at all. But the reality of success tells a different story. In almost every field, from technology to arts, from business to personal development, the people who achieve the most remarkable results aren't those who wait for perfection. They're the ones who take action, learn from real-world feedback, and adjust their course based on actual experience rather than theoretical perfection.

Hoffman's story isn't just about launching a technology platform; it's about the crucial choice we all face when pursuing our goals: wait for perfection or take action now. It's about understanding that the path to excellence isn't paved with perfect steps, but with consistent, imperfect action. The success of LinkedIn didn't come from its perfect launch, but from its ability to evolve through real-world feedback and continuous improvement—something that could only begin once it was released into the world.

The journey from paralysis to progress begins with understanding that perfect isn't just the enemy of good. It's the enemy of done, of started, of tried, and ultimately, of success itself.

The allure and pitfalls of perfectionism

From our earliest days, we're taught that excellence matters. Our teachers praise flawless test scores, coaches demand perfect form, and parents beam with pride at straight As. In professional life, this pursuit of excellence becomes even more embedded. Companies promise "best-in-class" solutions, law firms boast of their "meticulous attention to detail", and consulting firms sell their ability to optimise everything they touch. This relentless drive for quality has built remarkable organisations and launched countless successful careers.

As a consultant and manager, I have learnt firsthand the value of having exacting standards. The ability to spot imperfection, to see the gap between what is and what could be, is an essential skill in our profession. This "perfectionist eye" helps identify opportunities for improvement, efficiency gains, and innovative solutions. It's what clients pay for: our capacity to recognise flaws others might miss and envision better possibilities. Yet within this pursuit of excellence lurks a danger: perfectionism. While they might appear similar on the surface, perfectionism and high standards are fundamentally different. High standards drive us toward achievement; perfectionism often prevents it entirely.

I witnessed this distinction most starkly in a consulting project that never made it past the planning phase. What began as a few days of initial planning extended to weeks, then months. Plans were drawn up, critiqued, scrapped, and started again. The entire project budget was eventually consumed not by implementation but by the endless pursuit of the "perfect" solution. Looking back, there were numerous viable approaches that could have delivered real value—all rejected because they fell short of an impossible ideal.

The distinction becomes clear when we examine their different impacts.

High standards mean setting ambitious but achievable goals, focusing on continuous improvement, and maintaining rigorous quality without sacrificing progress. A consultant with high standards delivers thorough analysis and well-crafted recommendations while recognising that some degree of uncertainty is inevitable in any business decision.

5. Start before you're ready

Perfectionism, in contrast, sets impossible standards that no human could consistently meet. The perfectionist consultant might refuse to make recommendations until every possible scenario is analysed, every data point is triple-verified, and every potential objection is pre-emptively addressed. The result? Analysis paralysis, missed opportunities, and solutions that arrive too late to be relevant.

Early in my career, my ability to spot problems and propose solutions was a tremendous asset. But gradually, this skill became a burden. My brain became wired to see flaws in everything, not just in client work, but in every aspect of life. Each imperfection I identified became not just an opportunity for improvement but evidence of inadequacy. The more I achieved, the more harshly I judged myself for not achieving more.

This is perfectionism's cruellest trick: turning our drive for excellence into a weapon against our own self-worth. The very capability that makes us effective in our professional roles can become a lens that magnifies flaws while filtering out accomplishments. I've had to consciously retrain myself to recognise when this pattern emerges and to distinguish between helpful critical analysis and destructive perfectionist thinking.

But how can you recognise when healthy high standards have morphed into destructive perfectionism? I think there are a few warning signs:

1. Excessive research and planning

- You spend more time planning than doing.
- You feel you can never know enough to start.

- You constantly seek one more source, one more opinion.
- Your research becomes a form of procrastination.

2. Inability to complete or ship work

- Projects remain perpetually "almost ready".
- You revise endlessly without substantial improvement.
- You struggle to declare anything "done".
- Good solutions are rejected in pursuit of perfect ones.

3. Delegation difficulties

- You reflexively take on work others could do.
- You spend excessive time reviewing others' work.
- You frequently redo tasks others have completed.
- You struggle to trust teammates with important work.

4. Over-preparation and analysis

- You create contingency plans for unlikely scenarios.
- You spend disproportionate time on minor details.
- You analyse options long after sufficient information is available.
- You seek certainty in situations where it's impossible.

5. Self-worth tied to performance

- Small mistakes feel catastrophic.
- Success brings little satisfaction because it could have been "better".
- You take constructive feedback as personal criticism.

- You judge yourself more harshly than you would judge others.

Our professional culture not only accepts but often celebrates perfectionist tendencies. In job interviews, candidates knowingly cite "perfectionism" as their greatest weakness, aware that employers will likely interpret this as a strength. After all, who wouldn't want a team member who holds themselves to the highest standards? Corporate cultures reinforce this through performance reviews that focus on closing gaps, improvement plans that target deficiencies, and reward systems that celebrate exceptional achievement.

Yet as I've learnt through my own journey of retraining my perfectionist tendencies, maintaining high standards doesn't require this self-destructive pursuit of perfection. The key lies in recognising the difference between striving for excellence and demanding infallibility. High standards inspire us to do our best work while accepting that "best" doesn't mean "perfect". They push us to excel while acknowledging human limitations. Perfectionism, in contrast, demands an impossible standard that paralyses progress and crushes creativity.

The challenge, then, is maintaining the drive for excellence while preventing it from transforming into perfectionism's paralysis.

Perfectionism fuels your fear

The perfectionist sets standards so high that failure becomes virtually guaranteed. After all, if anything short of perfection is considered a failure, then by definition, almost everything will fail.

This elevated failure rate then reinforces the perfectionist's fear, leading to even higher standards or complete avoidance. And the most common consequence is inertia. When perfection is the only acceptable outcome, starting becomes nearly impossible. Think about writing a book. A healthy approach accepts that the first draft will be rough—it's a necessary step toward the final product. But the perfectionist, imagining only the flawless final version, becomes paralysed. How can you write the first word when every word must be perfect?

Even more problematic is what happens when perfectionists do manage to act. Because their standards are so high, normal setbacks feel like catastrophic failures. A programmer with perfectionist tendencies might see a minor bug as evidence of their fundamental inadequacy. A manager might interpret constructive feedback as proof they're unfit to lead. Each perceived failure hits harder because it's measured against an impossible standard.

This heightened experience of failure creates what psychologists call "learnt helplessness"—a condition where people become so convinced of their inability to succeed that they stop trying altogether. Consider these common manifestations:

- the entrepreneur who endlessly refines their business plan but never launches
- the artist who has dozens of nearly finished works but never shows them
- the professional who turns down promotions because they're "not quite ready"
- the writer who researches endlessly but never starts writing.

5. Start before you're ready

In each case, perfectionism doesn't prevent failure—it prevents success by preventing action entirely and the psychological cost is enormous. Each opportunity avoided becomes a regret. Each unfinished project becomes evidence of inadequacy. The perfectionist's world gradually shrinks as they retreat from challenges that might result in anything less than perfection. The fear of failure, rather than failure itself, becomes the primary obstacle to achievement.

But there's hope in understanding this dynamic. Once we recognise how perfectionism amplifies our fear of failure, we can begin to break free from its grip. The antidote isn't lowering our standards or accepting mediocrity—it's embracing action over perfection. It's understanding that progress, not perfection, is the path to excellence.

Action as the ultimate antidote

In our quest for perfection, we often forget a fundamental truth: action isn't optional—it's the only thing that truly matters. No amount of planning, analysis, or preparation can replace the simple necessity of doing.

I once taught swimming to young children. Our approach was remarkably simple: we got in the water immediately. No lengthy explanations of hydrodynamics, no complex discussions of technique. We simply began. The children would enter the pool, feel the water's buoyancy, experience how their bodies moved in this new environment, and gradually develop comfort and confidence through direct experience.

Imagine trying to teach swimming any other way. Picture spending months on theory, showing videos, drawing diagrams, and planning the perfect stroke—all while never touching the water. It sounds absurd when applied to teaching children to swim, yet this is exactly how many of us approach our professional challenges and personal goals. We plan, analyse, and prepare endlessly, forgetting that at some point, we simply need to get in the water.

Children intuitively understand the importance of action. Watch a child learn anything new—whether it's riding a bike, drawing, or playing a game. They don't wait until they've mastered the theory; they jump in and start doing. Their learning comes through action, through trial and error, through the direct experience of what works and what doesn't. Somewhere along the way to adulthood, many of us lose this natural inclination toward action, replacing it with an often-paralysing need to "get it right" before we begin. Yet action remains the most powerful antidote to perfectionism.

When we act, several powerful things happen:

1. **We get real feedback:** As we explored earlier in our discussion of failure as feedback, actual experience provides information that no amount of planning can replicate. Each action, whether successful or not, tells us something valuable about what works and what doesn't. This real-world feedback is far more valuable than theoretical planning.

2. **We build momentum:** Action creates momentum. Each step forward, no matter how small, makes the next step easier. This is why productive people often talk about the importance of "starting small". The size of the initial action matters less than the fact that you've begun moving forward.

3. **We experience achievement:** Even small accomplishments provide a sense of progress that theoretical preparation never can. This feeling of forward movement, of actually doing something, creates positive reinforcement that can help overcome the paralysis of perfectionism.

4. **We find joy in doing:** There's a satisfaction in actual work that planning can never provide. Whether it's writing, building, creating, or solving problems, the act of doing often brings its own rewards. Many perfectionists forget this simple pleasure in their endless pursuit of the perfect outcome.

5. **We learn through experience:** No amount of planning can replace the learning that comes from direct experience. Just as our young swimmers learnt more in five minutes of being in the water than they would from hours of poolside instruction, we learn more from doing than from endless preparation.

I think a great example of what businesses can gain through an action-oriented approach is the Virgin Group that embodied this principle through Richard Branson's famous "Screw It, Let's Do It" philosophy. When launching Virgin Atlantic in 1984, Branson had virtually no aviation experience—just a frustrating cancelled flight and the wild idea that he could create a better airline. Rather than spending years studying the industry or developing the perfect business plan, he leased a single Boeing 747 and jumped into the fiercely competitive airline business. When Virgin entered the mobile phone business, telecommunications giants scoffed at their lack of industry experience. But by starting before they were "ready" by industry standards, they brought fresh perspectives that led to customer-friendly innovations like rolling over unused minutes and eliminating long-term contracts—changes the established players hadn't considered despite their decades of experience and planning.

"If somebody offers you an amazing opportunity but you are not sure you can do it, say yes—then learn how to do it later," Branson advises. This approach has led Virgin into over 400 companies across diverse industries from music to telecommunications to space travel. In each case, Branson and his team learnt crucial lessons through action that no amount of theoretical preparation could have provided.

This isn't an argument for reckless action or against proper preparation. Virgin's success wasn't just about impulsive decisions. It was about recognising that at some point—usually much earlier than our perfectionist tendencies would prefer—we need to move from planning to action. The perfect moment to begin will never arrive. The perfect plan will never be complete. The perfect conditions will never exist.

Four power moves to get unstuck

Writing this book has been an exercise in confronting my own perfectionist demons. As someone who isn't a writer by training or profession, the thought of putting my words, thoughts, experiences, and insights out into the public domain was terrifying. Every sentence felt like it could be better, every chapter like it needed more research, every concept like it needed more refinement. The critic in my head kept asking: "Who are you to write this? What if it's not good enough? What if people find flaws in your arguments?" As a consultant, I'm used to polishing my work until it's bulletproof before presenting it to clients so this was not a new sensation, but a book is different. It's more personal, more visible, and feels more permanent. The perfectionist in me wanted to research endlessly, plan meticulously, and refine infinitely. Left unchecked, these tendencies would have ensured this book remained forever an idea, never becoming reality.

To move forward, I had to employ practical methods to overcome my perfectionist paralysis. Through trial and error, on this and other projects, I've discovered four specific techniques that helped transform my good intentions into actual progress. These aren't just theoretical concepts; they're tools that have helped me do many things. Here's how they work:

1. Limit planning time

The first step in breaking perfectionist paralysis is to put strict boundaries around planning activities. Without these constraints, planning can expand indefinitely, consuming all available time and energy while producing no actual progress. For this book, I had to set firm limits on research and outlining. It would have been easy to spend years reading every book ever written about failure, success, and human psychology. Instead, after a few failed attempts, I gave myself one month to complete initial research and create a working outline. Was this enough time to learn everything? Of course not. But it was enough to begin, and that's what mattered.

The key is to recognise that planning, while necessary, is fundamentally different from doing. Planning feels productive—you're taking notes, organising ideas, creating structures. But at some point, planning becomes a form of procrastination, a way to avoid the vulnerability of actual creation. By limiting planning time, we force ourselves to move from preparation to action.

2. Block time for doing

Ideas don't write themselves, businesses don't launch themselves, and projects don't complete themselves. Without dedicated time for action, even the best plans remain just plans.

Back to the book, this meant blocking out early morning hours specifically for writing. Not for research, not for outlining, not for editing—just for putting new words on the page. I had to be strict about this. When I sat down at the keyboard during these blocked hours, my only job was to write. The temptation to "just do a little more research" or "reorganise the chapter structure" was constant, but having this dedicated time for actual writing helped resist these perfectionist diversions.

The power of time-blocking lies in how it shifts the question from "Should I work on this now?" to "What work will I do during this time?" When the time is already committed, it bypasses the perfectionist tendency to delay until conditions are ideal.

3. Begin before you're ready

One of perfectionism's most convincing lies is that there will be a perfect moment to start—when you're fully prepared, when you have all the information, when conditions are ideal. This moment never arrives.

Writing this book meant embracing the discomfort of beginning before I felt ready. There were always more sources I could consult, more people I could interview, more examples I could gather. But at some point, I had to start writing actual chapters,

5. Start before you're ready

even though I knew they wouldn't be perfect. The sensation of not being quite ready became not a warning to wait, but a signal to begin.

This principle applies to any significant endeavour. The truth is, you'll never feel completely ready for anything important. The key is to recognise this feeling of unreadiness not as a barrier but as a normal part of the process—even a sign that you're pushing yourself toward meaningful achievement.

4. Reward action

To build sustainable momentum, we need to reward action rather than perfection. This means celebrating the act of doing, regardless of the outcome.

In writing this book, my reward system started small: the simple pleasure of a good coffee as I sat down to write each morning. This might seem trivial, but it created a positive association with the act of showing up and doing the work. I also kept a log of my daily word count, not to judge the quality but to celebrate the fact that I was acting consistently.

The key is to shift your focus from the quality of the outcome (which feeds perfectionist tendencies) to the consistency of action. Did you show up? Did you try? Did you put in the time? These become the metrics that matter, especially in the early stages of any project.

Launch today, perfect tomorrow

Take a moment to reflect on your own relationship with perfectionism. Perhaps you recognised yourself in the person who can't stop analysing, the entrepreneur who can't stop planning, or the creator who can't stop refining. Perhaps you saw your own patterns in the endless research, the over-preparation, or the difficulty in declaring something "done".

Now, consider this: every moment spent pursuing perfection is a moment stolen from progress. Every hour spent planning the perfect approach is an hour that could have been spent learning from actual experience. Every day delayed by the fear of imperfection is a day of potential growth lost forever. The cost of perfectionism isn't just measured in lost time or missed opportunities. It's measured in innovations never shared, businesses never started, books never written, and dreams never pursued. It's measured in the subtle but persistent erosion of our confidence, as the gap between our perfectionist standards and reality grows ever wider.

But there's hope in action. Remember Reid Hoffman launching an "embarrassing" version of LinkedIn that grew into a platform connecting millions. Think of every artist who ever shared an imperfect creation that moved someone deeply, every entrepreneur who launched before they felt ready and learnt through doing, every person who chose progress over perfection and found success not in flawlessness, but in forward motion.

The path forward is clear, though it may feel uncomfortable. Identify one area where perfectionism has been holding you back. Perhaps it's that project you've been planning for months without starting. Maybe it's the creative work you keep refining but never sharing. Or the business idea you've been researching endlessly without taking concrete steps to launch.

Now, take one imperfect action toward that goal. Do it today—not tomorrow, not when you feel ready, not when conditions are perfect. Do it now, knowing that imperfect action beats perfect inaction every time.

Remember, this isn't about lowering your standards. It's about recognising that true excellence emerges not from perfect individual actions, but from the cumulative effect of consistent, imperfect efforts. It's about understanding that mastery comes not from avoiding mistakes, but from learning through them. For now, your task is simple: take one imperfect action today. Let go of the need for perfection and embrace the power of progress. The journey from where you are to where you want to be doesn't require perfect steps—it just requires that you begin.

Key takeaways

- Fear of failure is often driven by perfectionism. Recognise when your desire for perfection is preventing you from starting.

- Defeat perfectionism by deliberately starting projects at 80% readiness rather than waiting for 100%, recognising that the final 20% of preparation rarely improves outcomes.

- Embrace strategic incompleteness by releasing early versions of your work to get real feedback, which is far more valuable than any amount of theoretical planning or anticipation.

- Limit planning time with strict boundaries (like setting a timer for 30 minutes) to prevent endless preparation from becoming a form of procrastination that delays actual progress.

The Failure Advantage

- Block specific time for action in your calendar—not for research, planning, or review—where your only job is to produce tangible work on your most important projects.

6.

The power of small wins

"Great things are done by a series of small things brought together." – Vincent van Gogh

I love watching people make terrible life decisions on *Grand Designs*. For the uninitiated, this British television show has been running since 1999, making it nearly as enduring as the architectural projects it follows. The format is simple: follow ambitious homeowners as they attempt to build their dream homes, while the eloquent host Kevin McCloud alternates between raised eyebrows of scepticism and poetic architectural metaphors. I'll admit, part of my fascination comes from the mix of inspiration and schadenfreude. There's something compelling about watching a bright-eyed couple declare they'll convert a 200-year-old water tower into a modern family home "within 12 months and on a tight budget", while Kevin gives his trademark knowing look to the camera. We viewers know what's coming: months of living in a muddy caravan, savings accounts draining faster than the perpetually flooded foundation, and at least one moment where someone breaks down over the cost of windows.

But beneath this seemingly formulaic television, I think *Grand Designs* offers an insight into how we view success, failure, and the messy space between. The show's grand reveals, those glossy, architectural-magazine-worthy final shots, are what we all wait for. We gasp at cantilevered glass boxes defying gravity, restored medieval barns embracing modernity, and eco-homes that look like they've sprouted from the earth itself. These moments of triumph are what make the show's YouTube compilations and architecture books.

Yet what makes *Grand Designs* truly special is its willingness to show the unglamorous reality of achievement. For every stunning final reveal, we've witnessed months (sometimes years) of mud-caked boots, rain-soaked timber, and countless "small" disasters that feel anything but small to those living through them. I remember one episode where a couple spent three weeks trying to get a curved steel beam just right—a detail that would be visible for perhaps two seconds in the final reveal, but without which the entire project would have failed. If the cameras stopped rolling during these moments of crisis—when the structural engineer is shaking their head, or when the custom-made windows arrive from Germany in the wrong size—every project would appear to be a failure. The neighbours driving past would see only a construction site haemorrhaging money and destroying the local view. Social media wouldn't get its perfect "after" photo. The reality is that every episode of *Grand Designs* is really a story about failure—dozens, perhaps hundreds of small failures, setbacks, and complications—until suddenly, it isn't.

This perfectly represents our modern relationship with achievement. We're obsessed with before-and-after transformations, overnight successes, and instant results. Even though *Grand Designs* packages years of work into 40 minutes of television, at least it shows us some of the mess in between. Those muddy boots and rainy days are precisely what we need to understand about success—that it's not a moment but a process, not a single triumph but a thousand tiny victories and setbacks.

Which brings us to a fundamental truth about failure and success: they aren't permanent states but rather snapshots taken at a particular moment in time. Too often, we declare failure prematurely, not realising that we're simply in the middle of our own *Grand Designs* episode—muddy boots and all. The real challenge isn't in avoiding failure but in recognising that those small setbacks are actually the building blocks of something greater. We just need the patience to let our own masterpiece emerge, one rain-soaked day at a time.

Compound your way to extraordinary results

Every remarkable achievement in human history, whether it's building the pyramids, writing a masterpiece, or breaking a world record, shares one fundamental truth: they are all the result of small gains accumulated over time. While we often celebrate the moment of triumph, the reality is that success is built piece by piece, increment by increment, in a process that harnesses one of the most powerful forces in nature: compound growth.

To understand this principle, consider a simple mathematical example. If you improve at something by just 1% each day, the mathematics of compounding means you'll be 37 times better by the end of the year. This isn't just theoretical; it's the hidden mechanism behind most forms of progress. Like a snowball rolling downhill, small initial gains build upon each other to create exponentially larger results over time.

This fundamental truth about progress also extends to human performance. Dr K. Anders Ericsson's research into expert performance revealed that what we often attribute to natural talent is actually the result of thousands of hours of deliberate practice; specific, focused effort aimed at improvement. His studies across diverse fields, from chess to music to athletics, consistently showed that elite performance isn't born, it's built through incremental progress. The evidence is everywhere once you know where to look. Michael Phelps' Olympic dominance wasn't achieved through one massive leap in ability, but through six hours of daily training from age 14 to 18, each session focused on minute improvements in technique. The Beatles' seemingly overnight success was actually the product of over 1,200 live shows, including marathon eight-hour sets in Hamburg clubs, where they refined their sound one performance at a time.

Yet despite understanding this principle, elite performance remains rare. I think the reason lies in a crucial caveat: while the mathematics of improvement is straightforward, the human element is not. Compound growth only works its magic through consistent application over time. The challenge isn't in understanding the principle, but in maintaining the effort required to achieve it. A 1% daily improvement sounds modest, but it demands sustained focus and energy. Elite performers aren't just willing to make small improvements; they're willing to make them day after day, year after year.

Overcome the motivation barrier

Understanding that success comes from small gains over time is one thing; sustaining the effort required to achieve those gains is quite another. Like a marathon runner facing mile after mile of pavement, the challenge isn't knowing what to do, it's finding the will to keep doing it, especially when the finish line seems so far away. This is where many of us stumble. We start with enthusiasm, committed to our goal of learning a new language, mastering a musical instrument, or transforming our organisation. But as days turn into weeks and weeks into months, our motivation wanes. The end goal remains distant, and our daily efforts can feel insignificant in comparison. We begin to question whether all this effort is really making a difference.

The answer to this motivational challenge lies in a simple but powerful concept: progress. In research conducted by Teresa Amabile and Steven Kramer, they analysed nearly 12,000 diary entries from knowledge workers and made an insightful discovery. Of all the things that can boost a person's motivation and emotional state during a workday, the single most important factor was making progress in meaningful work. Even small wins, tiny steps forward, had a surprisingly powerful effect on people's drive to continue. On days when people made progress, no matter how incremental, they reported higher levels of motivation, more positive emotions, and better perceptions of their work, their team, and their organisation. It wasn't just the major breakthroughs that mattered as even minor milestones provided a significant boost to people's inner work lives. One research participant showed this when they noted after solving a small but persistent bug in their code: "I smashed that bug that's been frustrating me for almost a calendar week. That may not be an event to you, but I live a very drab life, so I'm all hyped."

This provides us with a powerful tool for maintaining long-term motivation. Rather than focusing solely on the distant goal, we need to recognise and celebrate progress along the way. Each small step forward isn't just progress toward our goal; it's fuel for our motivation to continue. By acknowledging these incremental achievements, we create a virtuous cycle: progress breeds motivation, which in turn leads to more progress. The implications are clear for both personal achievement and team leadership. Rather than waiting for major milestones to acknowledge success, we should actively look for and celebrate small wins. Did you practise that instrument for 30 minutes today? That's a win. Did your team successfully resolve a minor technical issue? That's progress. These aren't just feel-good moments; they're crucial fuel for sustained effort.

This perspective also helps us reframe our relationship with failure. Small setbacks and failures along the way aren't just normal; they're an expected part of any meaningful journey. The only real failure would be to give up entirely. As Amabile and Kramer's research showed, while setbacks can temporarily dampen motivation, their negative effect is mitigated when we maintain our focus on progress and keep moving forward.

By recognising these small wins and maintaining our focus on progress rather than perfection, we can sustain the motivation needed for long-term achievement. Success doesn't come from avoiding failures or making huge leaps forward, it's about maintaining consistent forward momentum, one small step at a time.

Design systems that guarantee success

Understanding the power of incremental progress and generating motivation through small wins are essential for achievement. But relying on motivation alone rarely works. To sustain any effort over the long term, we need systems: reliable methods that ensure the work gets done regardless of how we feel on any given day. A system, whether personal or professional, reduces the daily drain of decision-making and willpower and creates a framework where progress becomes not just possible but probable, transforming sporadic effort into consistent action. Think of it as the difference between hoping to exercise and having an appointment with a trainer every Tuesday and Thursday at 7 a.m. The latter doesn't require you to rely on motivation each time; the decision has already been made, the pattern already established.

In our personal lives, habits can serve as these systems. When behaviours become habitual, they bypass the need for conscious decision-making and motivation, becoming as natural as brushing our teeth or taking a morning shower. The effort required to maintain these behaviours diminishes significantly once they're embedded in our daily routines.

In professional contexts, and within organisations, we need more structured systems; formal methods and processes that can coordinate the efforts of many people toward common goals. These systems provide frameworks for consistent improvement, ensuring that progress isn't left to chance or dependent on individual inspiration.

Harness the habit revolution

In recent years, our understanding of human behaviour has been revolutionised by insights into the role habits play in our lives. Through the work of researchers and authors like Charles Duhigg in *The Power of Habit* and James Clear in *Atomic Habits*, we've come to recognise that up to 40% of our daily actions aren't conscious decisions at all—they're habits, automatic behaviours that require little to no deliberate thought.

This recognition has profound implications for achievement. When we rely solely on motivation and willpower to accomplish difficult things, we're fighting against our brain's natural tendency to conserve energy. But when we create habits, we harness this tendency. Instead of requiring conscious effort and decision-making each time, habitual behaviours become automatic, like a program running in the background of our minds.

The beauty of habits lies in their efficiency. Once established, they dramatically reduce the mental energy required to take action. Consider the difference between having to decide each morning whether to exercise and having a routine where you automatically put on your running shoes at 6 a.m. The latter requires far less mental effort, making it more likely to happen consistently, especially on days when motivation is low. But habits aren't just about making things easier; they're about making hard things possible. By breaking down challenging goals into habitual daily actions, we create a sustainable path to achievement. Want to run a marathon? The habit of running three miles each morning will get you there. Want to learn a new language? Fifteen minutes of daily practice will accomplish more than sporadic cramming sessions.

The key to forming effective habits lies in understanding their structure. Every habit consists of a cue (trigger), a craving (motivation), a response (action), and a reward (satisfaction). By deliberately designing these elements, we can create habits that stick.

6. The power of small wins

Some proven strategies include:

1. making the cue obvious e.g. leaving your running shoes by the bed
2. making the action easy to start e.g. committing to just five minutes initially
3. making the reward immediate e.g. tracking your progress visually
4. stacking new habits onto existing ones e.g. "After I pour my morning coffee, I will write one paragraph."

To continue with my own experience writing this book, it was a daunting task that seemed overwhelming, and I had literally years of stopping and starting, writing, and rewriting. Some days I'd write hundreds of words and then I'd have weeks of not much activity—the self-imposed guilt of making no progress weighing me down until I found the time or motivation to push forward again. It wasn't until I formed a habit that I started to make consistent progress, and more words got committed to the page. For me, the order of implementation was a little different as I unknowingly used habit stacking first. For my entire adult life, I've been a relatively early riser and always enjoyed exercise of a morning—typically a run. I realised that this task, which seems difficult to some, came easily to me because it's just what I do. I set an alarm every day and get up and go for a run—without too much thought. This being the most reliable activity in my schedule I then put the writing alongside. I set the alarm a little earlier (making it easy to start), left the laptop out (the cue), and wrote some words before I went on my run. So, the new habit was write then run. True to the theory, I soon found that, after a few weeks, I had made substantial progress which felt good and allowed me to gradually increase the writing time and complexity.

By setting up this small, manageable habit, I created a system that moved me incrementally toward my goal. Whether I wrote 200 or 2,000 words in a session became less important than maintaining the habit of showing up each day. Over time, these small sessions accumulated into chapters, and chapters into a completed manuscript. The power of this approach lies not just in its effectiveness but in its sustainability. Rather than relying on bursts of inspiration or motivation, habits create a steady, reliable path to progress. They transform the question from "Will I write today?" to "When will I write today?" The action becomes not a choice to be made but simply part of who you are and what you do.

This is how habits become the bridge between knowing what to do and actually doing it consistently. They are the difference between having a goal and having a system to achieve that goal. When we build the right habits, progress becomes not just possible but inevitable—one small, automatic action at a time.

Master the kaizen advantage

While habits provide a personal framework for progress, organisations need more structured approaches to embed continuous improvement into their operations. Among the many systems developed for this purpose, few have proven as influential or effective as *kaizen*, the Japanese philosophy of continuous improvement that transformed manufacturing and has since influenced management practices across all sectors. Many now see *kaizen*, and its related methodologies such as "Lean", as systems of work that need to be implemented as complete frameworks with rigid

6. The power of small wins

ways of doing things, endless rules, and experts who advise on *the* method. But I think we can learn from the principles that make it successful whether or not one chooses to formally implement a particular methodology.

The roots of *kaizen* can be traced back to an unlikely source: America's World War II industrial mobilisation. In the early 1940s, as the United States redirected its industrial might toward the war effort, the nation faced a crucial challenge. With millions of inexperienced workers, including retirees, students, and farmers, joining the manufacturing workforce, the War Manpower Commission introduced the Training Within Industry (TWI Job Methods) programme. This system encouraged organisations to make small, immediate improvements while standardising jobs into closely defined steps that could be constantly refined.

The approach proved remarkably successful, helping America become the world's top industrial producer by 1945. After the war, during the American occupation of Japan, experts like Homer Sarasohn, Charles Protzman, W. Edwards Deming, and Lowell Mellen brought these methods to help rebuild Japanese industry. These Western ideas, combined with Japanese cultural values, evolved into what we now know as *kaizen*, which literally translates to "change for the better". The concept was further developed by Kaoru Ishikawa, a professor at the University of Tokyo, who expanded it into a comprehensive approach to business improvement.

The core principles of *kaizen* are deceptively simple:

- Every process can be improved.
- Many small improvements are more effective than a few big ones.

- Those closest to the work know best how to improve it.
- Progress comes through experimentation and learning.
- Success is measured by adherence to the improvement process itself.

What makes *kaizen* particularly powerful is its shift in focus from outcomes to process. Rather than fixating on grand transformations or breakthrough innovations, *kaizen* emphasises the cumulative impact of small, continuous improvements and sets the expectation that this will continue, forever. Success isn't measured by reaching a final destination (because there isn't one), but by maintaining consistent forward momentum through the improvement cycle.

This approach can fundamentally change how people engage with their work. When workers are empowered to identify and implement improvements in their daily tasks, they become more invested in the process. Employees in organisations practising *kaizen* principles report higher job satisfaction and engagement, which aligns with what we know about the progress principle—people feel more motivated and satisfied when they can see regular progress in meaningful work.

Toyota, perhaps the most famous practitioner of *kaizen*, demonstrates the power of this approach. Through their Toyota Production System, they institutionalised the process of continuous improvement, encouraging every employee, from assembly line workers to executives, to suggest and implement small improvements. The result? Toyota reportedly receives over a million improvement suggestions from employees annually, with an implementation rate over 90%. This commitment to incremental progress helped transform Toyota from a small local manufacturer into one of the world's largest and most respected companies.

Other organisations adopt similar principles in their own contexts. Intel uses a variation called "Copy Exactly" to maintain consistent quality while rapidly scaling production. Google's famous "20% time" policy, which encouraged engineers to spend one day a week on side projects, mirrors *kaizen*'s emphasis on continuous experimentation and improvement. Even healthcare organisations have successfully applied these principles to improve patient care and operational efficiency. What these examples share is a recognition that excellence isn't achieved through occasional bursts of transformation but through sustained, incremental progress. The focus isn't on reaching perfection but on getting better every day. This mindset shift is perhaps the most valuable lesson: there is no endpoint to improvement, only the ongoing process of making things better.

The success of *kaizen* demonstrates that when organisations create systems that support and celebrate incremental progress, they not only achieve better results but also create more engaging and satisfying work environments. It shows that the same principles that make habits effective on a personal level—consistency, small steps, and focus on process over outcomes—can be scaled to transform entire organisations.

Celebrate progress, not just outcomes

Having reoriented toward process, the next step to solving the motivation problem is *recognising* progress. In both personal and professional contexts, traditional achievement models focus almost exclusively on outcome milestones: completing the project, hitting the sales target, or reaching the weight goal. While these endpoints provide clear targets, they create motivational challenges for long-term endeavours. Process milestones, celebrating consistent behaviours rather than just results, provide psychological support for sustained effort and small-step approaches.

The fundamental challenge with outcome-based celebration is its infrequency. When success is defined solely by reaching the destination, the journey becomes merely something to endure rather than appreciate. This creates a feast-or-famine emotional cycle; long periods of strain punctuated by brief moments of satisfaction. Intermittent reinforcement is far less effective at sustaining motivation than regular recognition. Process milestones shift focus to the behaviours that ultimately produce results. Rather than celebrating only when you finish writing the book, you might celebrate completing 50 consecutive days of writing sessions. Instead of waiting until a business becomes profitable, you might recognise reaching 100 customer conversations. These process achievements acknowledge the discipline and consistency that make outcomes possible. I know I only really made progress on this book when I stopped worrying about when it would be finished and instead focused on how many words I was writing each day.

Effective process milestones share several characteristics. First, they focus on behaviours within your direct control rather than results influenced by external factors. Second, they emphasise consistency over intensity, rewarding regular practice rather than occasional heroic efforts. Third, they often involve round numbers or meaningful sequences that create natural moments of recognition and reflection. The power of process milestones extends beyond psychological encouragement. By celebrating behaviours rather than just outcomes, you reinforce the habits and systems that drive long-term success. This creates a virtuous cycle where recognition strengthens the very processes that generate results.

This approach is somewhat embedded in systems like *kaizen*, but organisations can also implement this through systematic recognition of process achievements. Software development teams might celebrate 50 consecutive days without a build failure. Manufacturing operations might recognise 1,000 hours without a safety incident. Sales teams might acknowledge 100 prospect conversations regardless of immediate conversion rates. Perhaps most importantly, process milestones make the small-steps approach sustainable by providing regular evidence of progress. They transform the experience from a seemingly endless journey toward a distant goal into a series of meaningful accomplishments. Each milestone becomes both a moment of recognition and a foundation for the next stage of advancement.

You too can do hard things, one step at a time

Back to our *Grand Designs* homebuilders, trudging through their muddy construction sites day after day, we can now better appreciate both their struggles and their path to success. Their story, like all stories of achievement, isn't really about the final reveal—it's about the accumulated impact of countless small actions, supported by systems that ensure progress, and motivated by visible steps forward. Success comes not from dramatic leaps forward but from the patient accumulation of small gains. Progress feeds motivation, which in turn drives more progress. And sustainable systems—whether personal habits or organisational practices like *kaizen*—ensure that progress continues even when motivation wanes.

Our deep need to see and celebrate progress reveals itself in curious ways. Consider the humble to-do list. While ostensibly a tool for tracking tasks, its true power often lies in the satisfaction of crossing items off. Many of us have experienced the peculiar pleasure of writing down a task we've already completed, just for the joy of immediately ticking it off. This isn't mere quirky behaviour—it's evidence of our fundamental need to recognise achievement, no matter how small. This insight offers us a new approach to tackling hard things. Rather than becoming overwhelmed by the magnitude of our goals or discouraged by setbacks along the way, we can focus on creating systems that support steady progress and celebrating small wins as they come. Whether writing a book, building a business, or transforming an organisation, the principle remains the same: break down the challenge into smaller pieces, establish reliable systems for progress, and maintain momentum through visible achievements.

This approach fundamentally changes our relationship with failure. When we understand that success is built from many small steps forward, temporary setbacks become not failures but natural parts of the journey. The only true failure becomes giving up entirely. Everything else is just feedback, information to help us adjust our course as we continue moving forward.

Key takeaways

- Break down ambitious goals into tiny, manageable actions that you can take daily—focus on 1% improvements rather than dramatic transformations, as these small gains compound dramatically over time.

- Create a habit-stacking system by attaching new desired behaviours to existing routines (like writing before your morning run), making the cue obvious and the initial action extremely easy to start.

- Track and celebrate small wins rigorously, as research shows that recognising incremental progress is the single biggest motivator for sustaining long-term effort and building positive momentum.

- Establish systematic routines that eliminate daily decision-making about whether to take action—schedule standing appointments and create default behaviours that happen automatically rather than relying on motivation.

- When building organisational change, consider *kaizen* principles or systems that focus on consistent progress rather than dramatic overhauls.

Part IV

Balance safety and challenge

On designing environments where risk-taking and excellence thrive together

Individual mindset shifts will only take you so far. The environments we work and live in shape our relationship with failure, either reinforcing fear or enabling growth. Creating the right conditions, for yourself and others, is the final piece of the failure advantage puzzle.

The most innovative and resilient teams maintain a delicate balance: psychological safety that makes risk-taking possible, alongside productive tension that drives excellence. By cultivating vulnerability that builds trust and embracing productive discomfort that challenges complacency, you'll create spaces where failure becomes a catalyst rather than a catastrophe. This environmental approach yields transformative benefits: increased innovation as people feel safe to experiment, faster problem-solving when issues are raised early without fear, deeper learning across the entire group from each individual's experiences, stronger resilience in the face of setbacks, and leadership at all levels as people take ownership of both successes and failures.

The Failure Advantage

Whether you lead a large organisation, a small team, or simply influence your immediate circle, these principles allow you to create conditions where the failure advantage becomes not just an individual capability but a collective strength. By deliberately shaping these environments, you multiply the impact of everything you've learnt and build cultures where people thrive precisely because they're unafraid to fail on the path to meaningful achievement.

7.
The courage to be vulnerable

"Experience is simply the name we give our mistakes."
– Oscar Wilde

The line between prudent decision-making and paralysing fear of failure can be remarkably thin. This truth became starkly apparent to me several years ago while advising two different organisations on implementing risk management frameworks. On paper, the situation couldn't have been more perfectly designed for comparison: two large companies, similar team sizes, identical objectives, and projects starting at the same time. The only significant difference? Their organisational cultures—and the profound impact this would have on their outcomes.

Both companies had recently faced operational disruptions that highlighted their need for better risk management. The initial phases progressed almost identically: teams were assembled, data gathered, problems analysed, and solutions designed. But when it came time to move from analysis to action, their paths diverged dramatically, revealing how deeply cultural attitudes toward failure can influence an organisation's ability to make progress.

The manufacturing company approached decisions with what I came to recognise as a "progress culture"." When we presented our proposal to their executive committee, they asked thorough questions and sought necessary clarifications. But crucially, their focus remained on forward momentum. The committee chair exemplified this mindset when I requested a follow-up meeting to address their questions. "Those don't need a meeting," she said matter-of-factly. "Resolve them with the individuals involved, and I'll get consensus via email." Within weeks, we had approval to proceed, with some sensible adjustments to the original plan.

The retail company, by contrast, had developed what I now understand was a "fear culture", though it masqueraded as thoroughness. Our initial presentation to their executive committee sparked reasonable questions, but this became the first of six identical cycles over the next year. Each meeting generated new questions, requiring more data, more analysis, more "what-if" scenarios. The questions became increasingly tangential, yet each needed to be exhaustively addressed before any decision could be made. "Risk management is everyone's responsibility" became the executive committee's refrain, a statement that sounds admirable but in practice meant everyone had input while no one had true ownership. The pursuit of perfect information became an excuse for inaction. When we spent a month collecting safety incident data from paper records, the discovery that timestamps were available led not to decisions but to requests for yet more analysis.

The contrast in outcomes was stark. Over twelve months, the manufacturing company implemented their framework, learnt from inevitable setbacks, and made meaningful progress toward their objectives. The retail company remained stuck in analysis, their fear of making the wrong decision preventing them from making any decision at all. The irony? When they finally moved

7. The courage to be vulnerable

forward, their solution barely differed from the original proposal—they had simply lost a year to fear disguised as diligence.

This experience with two cultures revealed an extraordinary opportunity as a leader. The way your team or organisation responds to the possibility of failure will shape everything from decision speed to innovation capacity to employee engagement. By transforming the cultural relationship with failure, you can unlock levels of performance and satisfaction that remain inaccessible to competitors trapped in fear-based thinking.

Think about the environments where you've done your best work. Chances are they weren't characterised by fear of making mistakes, but rather by a sense of psychological safety coupled with high standards. As a leader, you have the power to create these conditions for others, not through formal programmes or policies, but through how you personally respond to setbacks, the conversations you normalise, and the behaviours you consistently model.

The manufacturing company didn't succeed because they were reckless—they succeeded because their leadership created a culture that supported thoughtful action over endless analysis. They understood that some lessons can only come through experience, and that perfect information is often an illusion. By embracing this reality, they empowered their people to make meaningful progress while competitors remained paralysed.

Based on my own experience of being led and from observing both good and bad leadership examples I've found that five core leadership traits foster a failure-positive culture: vulnerability, curiosity, experimentation, responsibility, and positivity. These aren't specialised techniques you need to adopt solely to address failure but fundamental leadership qualities that create healthier, more effective organisations across all dimensions. By developing these traits, you'll not only transform your team's relationship with failure but also build an environment where people can do their best work and achieve results they never thought possible.

The aim: psychological safety and resilience

Before getting into the five leadership traits, we need to know what we're trying to achieve. The difference between our two companies wasn't just about decision-making processes or management styles. At its core, it reflected a fundamental distinction in psychological safety or the shared belief that team members can take interpersonal risks without facing negative consequences. In the manufacturing company, people felt safe enough to move forward with imperfect information. In the retail organisation, the absence of this safety led to analysis paralysis and delayed action.

Harvard professor Amy Edmondson, who pioneered research in this field, defines psychological safety as: "a belief that one will not be punished or humiliated for speaking up with ideas, questions, concerns, or mistakes." Her research, spanning over two decades, reveals something counterintuitive: the highest-performing teams aren't those with the fewest failures, but those where people feel safe enough to acknowledge and learn from their mistakes. Google's Project Aristotle, a comprehensive study to understand what makes teams effective, analysed hundreds of teams across the company. They found that psychological safety was by far the most important factor in team success—more important

7. The courage to be vulnerable

than individual talent, clear goals, or even team structure. The most effective teams weren't necessarily the ones with the most experienced members or the clearest processes. They were the ones where people felt safe to take risks, admit errors, and challenge assumptions.

You've likely experienced both psychologically safe and unsafe environments in your career. Think about a time when you made a mistake at work. In a psychologically safe environment, your first instinct might have been to share it with your manager, seek help in fixing it, and focus on what could be learnt. In an unsafe environment, you probably spent energy hiding the mistake, deflecting blame, or anxiously preparing defences for when it was discovered.

Or consider how innovation happens (or doesn't) in different team environments. In psychologically safe teams, people freely offer unconventional ideas, challenge established ways of thinking, and experiment with new approaches. In unsafe teams, people self-censor, offering only ideas they believe will be well-received, regardless of their potential value. This distinction plays out in countless ways. Teams with high psychological safety identify potential issues early, share bad news before problems escalate, find root causes rather than assigning blame, and collaborate across boundaries to solve complex challenges. They also demonstrate greater resilience, adapting quickly to changing circumstances, and learning continuously from both successes and failures.

Creating this environment isn't simply about being nice or avoiding difficult conversations. In fact, many outwardly polite

The Failure Advantage

workplaces lack psychological safety because their enforced politeness prevents candour. As Edmondson points out: "Candour is hard but non-candour is worse." True psychological safety enables honesty and productive challenge while maintaining respect for each person's value and contribution.

As an employee you probably know whether you feel safe in your work but as a leader how do you know what environment you are creating for your team? Clear signals include whether team members speak up in meetings (and who does the speaking), how mistakes are handled, whether people ask for help, and how dissenting views are treated. Try this simple test: when someone brings you bad news, how do you react? Is your first inclination to find out who was to blame or is it to focus on what can be learnt? Teams that focus on blame rather than learning are signalling that it's not safe to be imperfect.

Creating psychological safety isn't accomplished through policies or proclamations. It emerges from consistent leadership behaviours and team norms that demonstrate, rather than merely declare, that risk-taking and candour are valued. The most powerful way to build this environment is through how you, as a leader, model vulnerability, demonstrate curiosity, encourage experimentation, take responsibility, and maintain positive framing even in challenging circumstances. These five leadership traits, when consistently demonstrated, transform how teams approach challenges, respond to setbacks, and ultimately perform. Importantly, they're not specialised techniques you need to adopt solely to address failure—they're fundamental leadership qualities that create healthier, more effective organisations across all dimensions.

7. The courage to be vulnerable

Trait 1: lead through vulnerability

The word "vulnerability", until recently, wouldn't be found in business leadership manuals. In fact, many traditional leadership models view vulnerability as a weakness to be hidden rather than a strength to be leveraged. Yet in all my years of working with organisations across industries, I've observed that the most effective leaders, those who truly transform cultures and drive sustainable results, are often those who are willing to show their human side, acknowledge their limitations, and create space for others to do the same.

There is increasing evidence to confirm what many of us have experienced: vulnerable leadership creates better outcomes. Dr Brené Brown, whose research on vulnerability has transformed our understanding of leadership, defines vulnerability as: "uncertainty, risk, and emotional exposure." Her work reveals that vulnerability, far from being a weakness, is actually "our most accurate measurement of courage". Leaders who can embrace uncertainty and admit imperfection create environments where innovation and authentic engagement flourish.

Personally, I stumbled upon the power of vulnerability quite accidentally. Several years ago, I organised a development day for my team. The agenda was meticulously planned: a morning of reviewing annual objectives, followed by an afternoon of capability-building workshops. Everything was deliberately structured to demonstrate competence and control.

During lunch, sitting informally with the team, I mentioned something I hadn't planned to share: as a relatively new joiner to the organisation, I was finding it challenging to understand the complex organisational history and unwritten rules. I admitted feeling less effective than I wanted to be because I couldn't always understand the subtle dynamics at play in executive meetings or decode why certain decisions were made. It was a brief, unplanned moment of honesty, perhaps 10 minutes of conversation, before we moved on to the afternoon agenda. Yet in the weeks that followed, I noticed a change. Team members began checking in with me more frequently, offering unprompted explanations of organisational dynamics, and sharing their own stories of confusion or challenge. Small gestures appeared: a colleague forwarding me an email thread with added context, another inviting me to coffee to explain a particularly complex relationship between departments.

In hindsight this unplanned 10-minute conversation had more impact than the entire carefully designed day of development activities. By showing my own uncertainty, I had inadvertently set an implicit standard about what people could share and how they would be supported. I hadn't diminished my authority by admitting what I didn't know, I had actually strengthened my connection with the team and created an environment where authenticity became valued.

This experience taught me something profound about leadership: vulnerability connects at the level of hearts, not just minds. When we present ourselves as infallible, we may gain temporary admiration, but we create distance. When we acknowledge our humanity, struggles, uncertainties, and lessons learnt, we build bridges that enable true collaboration and growth.

The power of vulnerability in leadership lies in how it dismantles the fear of failure. When a leader demonstrates that they too

7. The courage to be vulnerable

have struggled, made mistakes, and continued to grow, it creates permission for others to do the same. The implicit message is powerful: "We value learning over perfection here. You don't need to hide your challenges or pretend to have all the answers. We grow together through honesty and shared experience." This manifests in several ways:

- acknowledging uncertainty when it exists rather than feigning confidence about ambiguous situations, creating space for others to contribute insights
- sharing relevant personal experiences, particularly around failure and learning, that normalise struggle and demonstrate growth
- creating safe spaces for others by responding supportively when they take risks, especially when they raise difficult issues or admit mistakes
- modelling continuous learning by actively seeking feedback, asking questions instead of always providing answers, and visibly changing course when new information suggests it's warranted.

The path isn't always comfortable, especially for those of us raised on traditional models of leadership that equate strength with certainty and command. Many worry that showing vulnerability might undermine their authority or expose them to criticism. Yet research and experience consistently show the opposite: leaders who demonstrate appropriate vulnerability are typically viewed as more authentic, more trustworthy, and ultimately more effective

As you consider your own leadership approach, ask your when was the last time your team saw you acknowledge take? How comfortable would you be saying: "I don't know, what do you think?" in a meeting? Do your team members see you actively learning and growing, or do they only witness polished performance? The answers to these questions may reveal opportunities to lead more vulnerably, and in doing so, to create the psychological safety that enables everyone to bring their best to work.

Trait 2: cultivate curiosity

While vulnerability opens the door to psychological safety, curiosity turns failure from a judgement into a learning opportunity. It shifts the entire conversation from "Who's to blame?" to "What can we learn?"—a fundamental reorientation that unlocks potential and drives growth. When we experience someone questioning our performance from a place of judgement, our biology and attention turns to threat responses and our cognitive resources become dedicated to self-protection rather than problem-solving. But when we encounter genuine curiosity, our brains respond differently—we remain in a state where creative thinking and collaboration are possible. This honesty is the foundation of genuine improvement. Curious leadership manifests in several key ways:

- asking questions that invite reflection and learning rather than defensiveness and blame
- listening with genuine interest to understand underlying causes rather than confirming existing assumptions
- treating unexpected outcomes with fascination rather than frustration, showing that surprises are valuable data

- replacing "why did you" with "what happened" to focus on understanding systems and contexts rather than assigning personal fault.

The beauty of curiosity is that it's contagious. When leaders respond to setbacks with genuine questions rather than accusations, they create a ripple effect throughout the organisation. Teams begin to approach problems differently, seeing them as puzzles to solve rather than failures to hide. This shift doesn't just feel better; it produces better results by unlocking the collective intelligence of the organisation.

When I first became a manager, I led a team that consistently missed delivery dates. My initial response was frustration as I had only ever needed to lead myself and I had assumed everyone worked like me. I questioned their commitment, capabilities, and work ethic. Predictably, this approach made the situation worse. Team members became defensive, problems went underground until they were major, and trust eroded. The turning point came when I started asking why? Rather than demanding explanations, I began asking genuine questions: "What obstacles are you encountering? What would help you move faster? What am I missing here?" The insights that emerged from these conversations were illuminating. I discovered unrealistic expectations, resource conflicts I hadn't been aware of, and process bottlenecks that could be easily addressed once they were visible. Not only did delivery performance improve dramatically, but team engagement and innovation increased as well. People who had been reluctant to raise issues now felt comfortable bringing problems forward early, when they were still manageable. Ideas flowed more freely because there was less fear of failure. The simple shift from judgement to curiosity had unlocked potential that had been there all along.

This approach doesn't mean abandoning accountability or accepting mediocrity. In fact, curiosity often leads to higher standards because it creates the conditions where honest assessment becomes possible. When people don't fear blame, they can be truthful about what's working and what isn't.

To build your capacity for curious leadership, start by noticing your own reactions to failure or setbacks. Do you immediately look for someone to blame? Do you feel the need to prove you weren't at fault? These are natural human responses, but they limit your effectiveness as a leader. Practise pausing in these moments and deliberately shifting to curiosity. What might you learn from this situation? What questions could reveal useful insights? Then, pay attention to how you communicate about failures with your team. Are your questions genuine inquiries or disguised accusations? "What were you thinking?" feels very different from "Help me understand your thinking." The first shuts down conversation; the second opens it up. By cultivating curiosity in your leadership approach, you create an environment where failure isn't something to fear but something to learn from. This doesn't just reduce anxiety; it fundamentally improves performance by ensuring that every setback contributes to future success.

Trait 3: embrace experimentation

"Would you rather be right, or would you rather be effective?" This question, posed by a mentor early in my career, captures the essence of experimental leadership. In a dynamic business environment, effectiveness often requires letting go of certainty and embracing a mindset of continuous testing and learning. The most innovative organisations rarely succeed through perfect planning or flawless execution. Instead, they thrive through deliberate experimentation—forming hypotheses, testing them quickly, learning from results, and adapting accordingly. This approach doesn't just produce better outcomes; it fundamentally transforms the relationship with failure by making it an expected, even valued, part of the innovation process.

Working with large customer service organisations I typically see two approaches to solving service problems. In some organisations the emphasis is on extensive upfront research, detailed requirements, and a comprehensive plan to build what they believe would be the perfect solution. They work diligently for months before revealing their solutions to customers, but in my experience often discover that they solved a problem customers didn't care about.

Other organisations take a more experimental approach. They quickly develop a rough prototype reflecting their initial hypothesis about customer needs, put it in front of users within weeks, and discover—just like the first team would later—that they had misunderstood the problem. But instead of this being a devastating failure, it is merely data point number one. They pivot, test a new approach, gather feedback, and iterate again. The second method nearly always results in solutions whilst the first always consumes effort but very often results in no change.

What's remarkable about this comparison isn't just that the experimental team gets to a better solution faster. It's how differently the two teams experience the process. The traditional team often feel demoralised by the eventual "failure", while the experimental team remain energised throughout, viewing each test as valuable learning rather than judgement on their abilities.

I often hear the critique that experimentation means chaos or abandoning planning entirely. However, for me, it's about approaching work with a scientific mindset—developing clear hypotheses, testing them systematically, and learning continuously. The best experimental leaders create structured approaches to testing and learning that make failure productive rather than threatening. Recall Amazon's "working backwards" approach that I highlighted in Chapter 3. When considering new initiatives, teams start by writing the press release they would issue if the product were successful. This forces them to clarify what success would look like from the customer's perspective. Then, rather than building the entire solution immediately, they identify the most critical assumptions underlying their vision and design experiments to test these assumptions as quickly and cheaply as possible.

Effective leaders apply an experimental mindset by:

- starting with hypotheses rather than certainties, approaching new initiatives with clearly articulated assumptions that can be tested
- designing small, fast experiments that deliver learning without requiring massive investments of time or resources
- celebrating valuable failures that deliver important insights, not just successful outcomes
- creating systematic approaches to capture learning from both successful and unsuccessful experiments.

7. The courage to be vulnerable

Developing an experimental leadership style requires overcoming deeply ingrained habits. Most of us were raised in systems that rewarded having the right answer, not asking the right questions. Our performance reviews typically focus on outcomes, not learning. And our organisational cultures often punish failure more than they reward intelligent risk-taking. Creating an experimental environment requires deliberate leadership choices. It means explicitly valuing learning alongside outcomes. It means creating psychological safety so people feel comfortable raising concerns and sharing lessons from unsuccessful attempts. It means designing work processes that include regular checkpoints for reflection and adaptation.

When you embrace experimentation, you give your team a tremendous gift: the freedom to try approaches that might not work, knowing that what matters isn't being right the first time but getting to the right answer eventually. This doesn't just reduce fear; it unleashes creativity, accelerates learning, and ultimately produces better results. The paradox of experimental leadership is that by becoming more comfortable with not knowing the answer in advance, you actually increase your chances of finding breakthrough solutions. By making it safe to fail in small, controlled ways, you dramatically reduce the likelihood of catastrophic failure later on. And by treating every outcome, successful or not, as a source of learning, you ensure that your team and organisation grow stronger with each attempt.

Trait 4: take ownership without blame

Few leadership traits transform an organisation's relationship with failure as fundamentally as the capacity to take clean, clear responsibility, without spiralling into blame or excessive self-criticism. This ability creates an environment where people can engage honestly with challenges, learn from mistakes, and maintain the energy needed for exceptional performance.

Business philosopher Fred Kofman calls this "unconditional responsibility": the willingness to focus on what you can influence rather than what's outside your control. It's not about assuming blame for everything that goes wrong but about approaching challenges from a stance of agency rather than victimhood. As Kofman puts it: "The price of innocence is impotence." When we focus on proving we're not at fault, we surrender our power to affect change.

Kofman articulates this distinction through what he calls the "victim" versus "player" mindsets. Those with a victim mindset focus primarily on factors outside their control. They view challenges as things that happen to them, seek to protect their ego through claimed innocence, and expend energy on assigning blame. This approach leaves them feeling powerless and fearful. In contrast, those with a player mindset concentrate on what they can influence. They see challenges as circumstances to navigate, build confidence through taking responsibility, and direct energy toward solutions rather than blame. This orientation leads to feelings of empowerment and motivation, even in difficult situations. He illustrates this brilliantly with an analogy that's both humorous and profound. Two people are riding an escalator when it suddenly stops. They stand there, complaining about their situation, shouting for help, becoming increasingly frustrated. The solution is obvious to observers: just walk up the remaining steps. Yet how often do we find ourselves metaphorically stuck on escalators in our professional lives, focusing on who broke the escalator rather than simply walking up the steps?

I can think of at least one example where I fell into this trap. The team had been working for months on a major client proposal, and we were confident we'd win the work. When the client called to tell us they'd chosen a competitor, my first instinct was defensive: the client hadn't fully understood our approach, the winning firm had unrealistically low-balled their price, our internal approval processes had slowed us down. These explanations weren't wrong, but they weren't useful. Having recently been exposed to Kofman's work, I consciously shifted to a stance of unconditional responsibility: "We lost this work. What could I have done differently?" This simple reframing changed the dynamic. Instead of feeling helpless or resentful, I felt empowered. I reached out to the client for feedback, discovered insights about our approach that would have remained hidden otherwise, and ultimately strengthened the relationship despite losing the initial project.

Responsible leadership manifests in several key practices:

- focusing first on your own contribution to problems before looking at others' roles, modelling that responsibility starts with yourself
- using "I" and "we" language when discussing setbacks rather than distancing language, like "they" or "the situation"

- addressing issues directly rather than allowing resentment or blame to fester
- distinguishing responsibility from blame, emphasising learning and future action rather than guilt or punishment.

This isn't just about individual outlook; it shapes entire organisational cultures. When, as a leader, you consistently model responsibility, it becomes the norm. Issues are raised earlier, problems are solved more efficiently, and relationships remain intact through difficulties. Contrast this with blame-oriented cultures where problems stay hidden until they're catastrophes, relationships deteriorate with each setback, and energy gets diverted to self-protection rather than problem-solving.

The most powerful aspect of responsible leadership is how it transforms the experience of failure from shame to learning. When people know they won't be blamed for honest mistakes, they're more willing to take reasonable risks, acknowledge when things aren't working, and share what they've learnt. This doesn't mean eliminating accountability—quite the opposite. True accountability becomes possible only when people feel safe enough to be honest about what's happened and their role in it. Kofman's framework goes further by distinguishing between "above the line" and "below the line" responses to challenges. Below the line responses focus on blame, excuses, and denial—the classic victim stance. Above the line responses acknowledge reality, take ownership of what can be influenced, and focus on moving forward constructively. This simple mental model provides a powerful tool for catching yourself when slipping into victim mode and consciously choosing a more empowered response.

Developing your capacity for responsible leadership starts with awareness. Notice when you slip into blame—of others or yourself. Pay attention to your language: "I couldn't because..." often signals a victim mindset, while "I didn't because..." acknowledges choice and agency. Practise reframing situations to focus on what you can influence rather than what you can't control. Then, examine how you respond when others bring problems to your attention. Do you immediately look for someone to blame? Do you get defensive if the issue might reflect on you? Or do you focus on understanding what happened and what can be learnt? Your response in these moments powerfully shapes your team's relationship with failure.

By modelling unconditional responsibility, you create an environment where failure loses its sting. It becomes not a threat to be avoided but a natural part of meaningful work—something to be learnt from rather than feared. This doesn't just improve results; it transforms the entire experience of work from a series of judgements to a journey of continuous growth and learning.

Trait 5: lead with contagious optimism

"You seem to talk about failure a lot," a colleague recently remarked after reading one of my blog posts. "Doesn't that create a rather negative environment?" His question revealed a common misconception about building failure-positive cultures, that acknowledging and learning from failure somehow means adopting a pessimistic worldview. In fact, I believe the opposite to be true. Creating an environment where failure can be discussed openly and learnt from requires a fundamentally optimistic perspective, one that sees possibilities rather than just problems.

Peter Drucker, the renowned management expert, identified this paradox decades ago when he observed that effective executives focus on opportunities rather than problems. "Problems have to be taken care of, of course," he noted, "But problem-solving, however necessary, does not produce results." This insight cuts to the heart of positive leadership in a failure-positive culture: we acknowledge and learn from failures not because we're pessimistic, but because we're optimistic about our ability to grow and improve. Research from Stanford psychologist Alia Crum further reveals just how powerfully our mindsets shape our reality. In one striking study, hotel housekeepers who were simply told their work constituted exercise, meeting surgeon general guidelines, showed physical health improvements compared to a control group—without changing their actual work. The only difference was their mindset about what they were doing. This has profound implications for how we lead through failure. When we frame setbacks as learning opportunities rather than threats, we literally change how people experience and respond to them.

In leading transformation projects I have had to adjust my own style over time and still need to consciously focus on this trait. My natural tendency is to highlight problems, risks, and potential failures. I think this is being thorough and responsible, but I am at risk of creating an environment of fear and paralysis. Team members may become hesitant to try new approaches, knowing their failures would be scrutinised. Innovation could slow. It wasn't until a mentor pointed out that my "realistic" approach may be perceived as pessimistic that I began to shift my leadership style. By consciously choosing to focus on possibilities rather than just problems, I see changes in how teams approach challenges. When

7. The courage to be vulnerable

something goes wrong—and things still go wrong—the conversation shifts from "Who's to blame?" to "What can we learn?" This isn't about ignoring problems or maintaining artificial cheerfulness. It's about maintaining a fundamental belief in our ability to learn and improve.

This shift requires consistent demonstration of specific behaviours. It means remaining calm and objective during crises and showing that setbacks aren't catastrophes. It means setting a positive tone in every interaction, recognising that people look to leaders for cues about how to respond to challenges. It means openly embracing uncertainty and ambiguity, acknowledging that not having all the answers is normal and acceptable. Perhaps most importantly, positive leadership means consistently finding opportunity in adversity. When a major project fails, positive leaders don't just analyse what went wrong; they help their teams identify what can be learnt and how these insights can improve future efforts. They celebrate progress and small wins, recognising that success usually arrives slowly, in increments that might go unnoticed without intentional attention.

This approach also extends to how we interpret others' actions. Positive leaders assume positive intent, recognising that most people come to work wanting to succeed and contribute. When someone makes a mistake or acts in ways that create problems, positive leaders seek to understand rather than condemn. They focus on process over outcome, recognising that mastery comes through continuous refinement rather than sporadic perfection. Making this work in practice requires careful attention to language and communication. Instead of asking: "Who's responsible for this mistake?" positive leaders ask: "What can we learn from this experience?" Instead of declaring: "This is unacceptable," they inquire: "How might we improve this process?" These aren't just semantic differences; they fundamentally shape how people think about and respond to failure.

The impact of positive leadership extends far beyond making work more pleasant. When people feel optimistic about their ability to learn from failure, they take smarter risks, collaborate more effectively, learn more quickly, and innovate more freely. This creates a virtuous cycle where each successful navigation of failure builds confidence for future challenges. The key is consistency. People don't judge leaders by their words but by their actions over time. Every interaction, every email, every meeting is an opportunity to demonstrate positive leadership and reinforce the culture you're trying to build. When leaders consistently demonstrate belief in possibility and growth, they create environments where failure becomes not something to fear, but something to learn from on the path to greater achievement.

Culture is built through daily actions

While each trait is powerful on its own, their true impact emerges when they work together to create a coherent culture where failure becomes not something to fear, but something to learn from. This cultural transformation doesn't happen through formal programmes or policies alone. As management expert Peter Drucker wisely observed: "Culture eats strategy for breakfast." The most beautifully crafted failure-tolerance initiative will falter if your daily behaviours as a leader contradict its principles. Conversely, consistently modelling these five traits will shape your team's culture even without formal declarations or programmes.

7. The courage to be vulnerable

In practice I see two common cultural challenges you may face when embarking on a new approach: organisations that give superficial attention to failure but undertake no real change, and those that do not accept failure as a concept at all, somehow thinking that denying its existence will prevent its occurrence.

An example of the former would be when some organisations create initiatives like a "Celebrate Failure" project, complete with workshops, posters, and a dedicated intranet portal. Yet when a major project encounters problems, senior leaders still demand to know "who screwed up", creating a clear contradiction between stated values and lived experience. These initiatives quickly became a cynical joke among employees.

In the case of the latter, some organisations hide behind impossible standards and statements of excellence to punish any setback that occurs. Taking a different view of failure in this environment can be particularly challenging as you may be fighting against a seemingly impossible tide.

My only advice in these situations is to model the five attributes above and seek to use them to change attitudes. When problems arise, acknowledging your own role (vulnerability) may invite others to do the same, asking genuine questions (curiosity) may reveal new insight and take the focus away from labelling the event as a failure or success, experimentation may introduce a new way of working, and remaining positive will start to demonstrate that a new way is possible. The desired result? A culture where people feel safe bringing up problems early, learning is valued as much as success, and innovation flourishes. Consistent with the concepts in this book, you will never know whether an organisation is truly resistant to change until you take action and treat every setback as a data point for the next step.

The key insight here is that culture lives in the thousands of small moments that make up organisational life, how leaders respond when someone admits a mistake, what gets celebrated in team meetings, which behaviours are rewarded, and how setbacks are discussed. These moments matter far more than formal declarations about culture.

Give your team the failure advantage

By cultivating the five leadership traits we've explored, you can transform this relationship in your own team or organisation.

When you lead with vulnerability, showing your own human side and acknowledging your limitations, you create permission for others to do the same. When you approach challenges with genuine curiosity rather than judgement, you transform failure from something to hide into something to learn from. When you embrace experimentation, treating work as a series of testable hypotheses rather than perfect plans, you make failure a natural and valuable part of the innovation process. When you take responsibility, focusing on what you can influence rather than what's outside your control, you model a stance of agency rather than victimhood. And when you lead positively, maintaining belief in possibility even during setbacks, you help others see failures as temporary and specific rather than permanent and defining. Together, these leadership traits create an environment where people can bring their full capabilities to work without fear that mistakes will define them. This doesn't just feel better; it produces better outcomes by unlocking creativity, accelerating learning, and building resilience.

7. The courage to be vulnerable

The ultimate paradox of failure-positive leadership is that by making it safe to fail in small, productive ways, you dramatically reduce the likelihood of catastrophic failure. Organisations that can learn quickly from small setbacks rarely experience the kind of major failures that bring down companies. Teams that can speak honestly about problems solve them before they become crises.

As a leader, you have the power to create this environment for your people. You can free them from the paralysis of perfectionism, the energy drain of hiding mistakes, and the limitation of playing it safe. You can release the tremendous potential that exists in every organisation but often remains locked away by fear of failure. This transformation begins not with grand pronouncements or formal programmes, but with how you show up tomorrow. How will you respond the next time someone brings you bad news? What questions will you ask when a project goes off track? Where might you show more of your own humanity to create space for others to do the same?

The path to building a failure-positive culture isn't always easy or comfortable, but it's one of the most powerful ways you can serve your organisation and the people in it. By changing your relationship with failure, you don't just become a more effective leader. You create an environment where everyone can do their best work, learn continuously, and find meaning in the journey of growth rather than just the destination of success.

Key takeaways

- Model vulnerability by openly sharing your challenges and lessons learnt to create psychological safety where team members feel comfortable taking risks and admitting mistakes.

- Replace blame-focused questions with curiosity-driven inquiries, like "What happened?" and "What can we learn?", to transform failures into valuable learning opportunities.
- Implement small, rapid experiments with clear hypotheses instead of perfect plans to accelerate learning and normalise failure as part of the innovation process.
- Take unconditional responsibility by focusing on what you can influence rather than assigning blame, demonstrating that accountability is about learning and improvement, not punishment.
- Maintain a consistently positive outlook when setbacks occur by highlighting possibilities for growth and celebrating small wins to build team resilience and encourage smart risk-taking.

8.
Embrace productive discomfort

"Character cannot be developed in ease and quiet. Only through experience of trial and suffering can the soul be strengthened, ambition inspired, and success achieved."
– Helen Keller

Throughout this book, we've explored how fear of failure can paralyse us, how perfectionism can prevent progress, and how embracing failure as feedback can accelerate our growth. I've advocated for creating environments where failure is accepted, even celebrated, as a necessary part of innovation and learning. But here, in our final chapter, I'm now at risk of contradicting myself: complete freedom from the fear of failure might be as detrimental as being paralysed by it.

Let me start with a story to explain.

In 1908, in a small laboratory at Harvard University, two researchers made a peculiar discovery while conducting experiments with Japanese dancing mice. Robert Yerkes and John Dodson were investigating how different intensities of electric shock might affect learning. Their seemingly simple experiment—training mice to choose between black and white boxes—would reveal something about performance that extended far beyond their intention. What they discovered was both counterintuitive and revolutionary: the relationship between stress and performance wasn't linear. Mice that received very weak shocks learnt slowly. Those that received moderately strong shocks learnt faster. But here was the surprise. Mice subjected to the strongest shocks actually performed worse than those receiving moderate stimulation. This pattern formed what is now known as the Yerkes-Dodson law, represented by an inverted U-shaped curve that shows performance peaking at moderate levels of arousal and declining when arousal is either too low or too high.

I think this finding tells us something important about how we need to experience failure. Just as Yerkes and Dodson's mice needed some level of motivation to learn effectively, we too need a certain productive tension in our work and lives. Without any concern for outcomes, we risk falling into complacency or mediocrity. Without any standards against which to measure our efforts, we might mistake motion for progress. The key isn't to eliminate all anxiety about failure, but to find that optimal zone where we feel enough tension to perform at our best while remaining free enough to take intelligent risks.

Consider a pianist preparing for a major performance. Too much anxiety about potential failure can lead to paralysis, frozen fingers, and forgotten sections. But too little concern might result in a technically correct but soulless performance, lacking the edge that comes from pushing boundaries. The best performances often come from finding that sweet spot where the musician is both relaxed enough to access their skills and engaged enough to transcend mere competence. This principle plays out across all domains of human achievement. The most innovative companies maintain enough structure to ensure quality while creating space for experimentation. The most effective leaders balance high standards with psychological safety. The most successful entrepreneurs combine bold vision with pragmatic execution.

Strike the perfect balance

Despite my belief in a failure-positive attitude, I'm opposed to failure becoming trivialised. Throwaway catchphrases, like "it's ok to fail" and "fail fast, fail often", not only minimise the whole topic but also carry a hidden danger. While they aim to reduce the paralysing fear of failure that prevents innovation and growth, they can inadvertently create a different problem: the normalisation of failure to the point where it loses its power to teach and motivate.

Technology companies are famous for embracing these mantras, but not all do so trivially. Consider two companies facing product defects. Company A, having fully embraced the "fail fast" philosophy, treats the defect as just another expected bump in the road. They acknowledge it casually, make quick fixes, and move on. Company B maintains a more nuanced relationship with failure. They accept that defects will occur but treat each one as a significant event worthy of deep analysis and learning. They don't panic, but they don't shrug it off either. Fast forward and Company A is likely to accumulate a pattern of similar defects, while Company B will systematically eliminate entire categories of potential failures. The difference lies not in their acceptance of failure, as both companies understand it's inevitable, but in how they maintain productive tension with failure.

The Steve Jobs story again proves insightful here when we consider Apple under Steve Jobs versus Apple under John Sculley in the mid-1980s and early 1990s. It is often observed that under Sculley's leadership, Apple adopted what many would consider a more "reasonable" approach to product development. The company became more process-oriented, more accepting of compromise, and more tolerant of imperfection. This more relaxed attitude toward failure led to a proliferation of products, including printers, digital cameras, and various Macintosh models, with overlapping features. While none of these products were outright failures, they lacked the excellence that had previously defined Apple. In contrast, Jobs maintained what he called "insanely high standards". This didn't mean he was afraid of failure—indeed, his return to Apple in 1997 was marked by numerous bold, risky decisions. But he never allowed failure to become normalised. When products fell short of expectations, it mattered. Each setback was treated not as an acceptable outcome but as an opportunity for profound learning and improvement. This productive tension led to a string of revolutionary products, from the iMac to the iPhone.

The key difference wasn't that one approach accepted failure and the other didn't. Rather, it was about maintaining the right relationship with failure. Jobs understood that while failure shouldn't be crippling, it should hurt a little. That discomfort—properly managed—drives learning, innovation, and excellence. There are mixed views on whether Jobs got the balance right, but this goes to show the inherent challenge.

The danger of fully normalising failure becomes particularly apparent in high-stakes environments. A hospital that becomes too comfortable with surgical complications, a financial institution that grows cavalier about risk management, or an airline that becomes accepting of near misses. We need enough productive

8. Embrace productive discomfort

tension to maintain the focus on quality, so the challenge is to find the balance: creating enough psychological safety that people are willing to take intelligent risks while maintaining enough productive tension that failure retains its power to motivate and teach. This means:

- accepting failure as inevitable while never becoming comfortable with it
- creating safe spaces for experimentation while maintaining high standards for final delivery
- treating failure as a teacher without letting it become a regular guest
- understanding that not all failures are equal—some should hurt more than others
- maintaining different standards for exploration versus execution.

The goal isn't to eliminate failure but to make it productive.

Target your optimal performance zone

Just as elite athletes speak of being "in the zone", that sweet spot between relaxation and focus where peak performance occurs, I believe there exists a target zone in our relationship with failure. Finding it requires understanding both the science of performance and the psychology of growth. Research across multiple fields points to the existence of this optimal zone. In sports psychology, it's known as the Individual Zones of Optimal Functioning (IZOF). In cognitive psychology, studies of "productive perfectionism" versus "neurotic perfectionism" reveal how different forms of self-criticism affect performance. Perhaps most compellingly, Teresa Amabile's research into creativity and innovation identifies what she calls the "Goldilocks Zone" of challenge—where tasks are neither so easy that they breed complacency nor so daunting that they trigger paralysis.

Again, in writing this book, and the many scrapped drafts that came before it, I experienced this spectrum. In starting out I approached it with what, in hindsight, could be considered neurotic perfectionism. Each sentence had to be flawless before I moved to the next. I'd spend hours agonising over word choice, often deleting entire paragraphs in fits of self-doubt. While the writing was technically sound, I produced little and reading those sections back later I found they were so edited as to have become bland. It wasn't until I talked to writers and to read about the writing process that I found a better way. A key turning point for me was when I read about the concept of a "vomit draft", popular in screen writing where the author simply dumps out all their thoughts on a page without ever going back and editing or worrying about whether it made sense—that was a job for editing. I needed to understand and embrace the fact that the first draft would be messy. Suddenly I had words on a page to work with and, on good days, the initial draft would contain some of the best sections. There is no way I would ever share this vomit draft with the world, so I still had the necessary tension to drive ultimate quality, but I had found a way to not stifle creativity. The difference in process was not in my standards, as I care deeply about quality, but in my relationship with imperfection. In the first case I saw imperfection as unacceptable, but later I saw it as a necessary step toward excellence.

8. Embrace productive discomfort

Based on this, I think the target zone has several key characteristics:

1. Balanced tension
- enough stress to maintain focus and drive improvement
- not so much that it triggers avoidance or paralysis
- a dynamic state that requires constant adjustment.

2. Clear standards
- well-defined criteria for success
- recognition that different stages require different standards
- understanding the difference between experimentation and execution.

3. Learning orientation
- focus on growth rather than judgement
- quick recovery from setbacks
- ability to extract lessons from failures.

4. Productive discomfort
- comfort with being uncomfortable
- recognition that growth happens at the edges
- ability to distinguish between destructive and constructive pain.

5. Flexibility
- different standards for different contexts
- ability to shift between experimental and performance modes
- recognition that the target zone changes as skills improve.

Finding your target zone is highly individual and a key reason that good leadership remains an art form. What feels like productive tension to one person might be paralysing to another. Studies of "productive perfectionism" reveal that high standards can enhance performance when coupled with:

- self-directed goals rather than externally imposed ones
- focus on personal growth rather than social comparison
- ability to maintain perspective about failures
- clear distinction between standards and self-worth.

Amabile's research also offers us a way to understand how organisations can help their people thrive in that elusive target zone. Through her extensive studies, she discovered that progress in meaningful work stands as the single strongest motivator in professional life. So, this isn't just about accumulating wins; it's about calibrating the journey perfectly.

    Consider how this calibration plays out in different professional contexts. In software development, the target zone shifts dramatically between environments while maintaining a consistent commitment to quality. Testing environments typically embrace a culture where failure isn't just tolerated; it's expected and valued. "Break it now so it doesn't break later" becomes the operating principle. Developers intentionally try to crash systems, inject faulty data, and stress-test applications to their limits, often with an almost playful energy as they compete to find vulnerabilities. But when the same team shifts to production deployment, the approach transforms completely. The casual experimentation gives way to checklists, multiple approvals, and careful monitoring. The tolerance for error drops dramatically, but importantly, the core commitment to quality remains constant. Successful development teams master this art of shifting their target zone while preserving their fundamental values.

Creative fields demonstrate similar patterns in their workflow phases. During early brainstorming for a new campaign or project, the emphasis typically falls on maximum openness with minimal judgement. "There are no bad ideas in brainstorming" serves as more than just a management expression, it creates space for unexpected ideas to emerge. As projects progress toward refinement stages, standards gradually tighten. What was once celebrated as "interestingly unconventional" might now be scrutinised as "off-strategy". By final production, every element undergoes intense scrutiny against elevated standards.

The secret to finding and maintaining your target zone isn't about establishing a fixed standard and rigidly adhering to it. Rather, it resembles the constant adjustments of a dial, sensing the environment and making subtle corrections to maintain the optimal quality. When signs of complacency appear—tasks becoming too routine, challenges feeling too comfortable—it's time to turn up the heat by introducing new challenges, raising standards, or pushing boundaries. Conversely, when anxiety spikes and productive tension transforms into paralysing stress, it's time to dial back. Breaking tasks into smaller components, focusing on process over outcomes, or revisiting fundamentals can help restore balance.

Personal growth lies on the edge of competence

I still remember my first driving lessons. Sitting behind the wheel, everything felt overwhelming—the sensitivity of the steering, the pressure needed on the pedals, the constant stream of decisions about speed and position. The simple act of driving, which I'd watched others do effortlessly thousands of times, suddenly seemed impossibly complex.

Fortunately, my father and brother understood something I would only later recognise: real learning happens at the edge of our current abilities. They didn't throw me straight onto busy streets or expect me to master everything at once. Instead, they carefully constructed a learning journey that kept me in what psychologists call the "learning edge"—that sweet spot between comfort and panic where growth occurs. We started in an empty parking lot with an automatic transmission. Just starting the car, moving forward, and stopping. Once those basics became comfortable, we progressed to quiet suburban streets where I might encounter the occasional oncoming car. Then to busier roads, adding parking manoeuvres at the end of each lesson. Finally, we switched to a manual transmission—a change that sent me back to the parking lot to rebuild my confidence with this new complexity.

At each stage, I felt a peculiar mix of nervous energy and eager anticipation. The tasks were challenging enough to demand my full attention but not so difficult that they felt impossible. Looking back, I can see how masterfully my teachers managed this progression (though I suspect they applied more common sense than science!). They kept me working at the edge of my competence—that narrow band where real learning occurs.

8. Embrace productive discomfort

This "learning edge" is a phenomenon well-documented in education. It lies just beyond our current capabilities but before the point where tasks become overwhelming. As sports psychologist Jeff Mitchell explains, it's the zone where we're challenged enough to stay engaged but not so challenged that we shut down from anxiety. When we operate here, we make mistakes—but they're productive mistakes that lead to growth rather than devastating failures that cause us to quit.

The learning edge has several key characteristics:

- Tasks are just beyond current mastery.
- Mistakes are frequent but manageable.
- Progress feels challenging but possible.
- Feedback is immediate and actionable.
- Motivation comes from visible improvement.

Today, my driving skills have plateaued. Like most experienced drivers, I've reached a level of competence that allows me to navigate daily traffic without much conscious thought. This is fine for driving, as we don't all need to be Formula One racers, but it illustrates a crucial point about growth and development. Once we stop operating at our learning edge, our skills stop improving. This plateau effect can occur in any area of life—professional skills, relationships, personal development. When we get comfortable, when tasks become routine, we stop growing. The path to continued development requires us to deliberately seek out challenges that push us back to that productive edge of discomfort.

Consider how different my driving journey might have been if my teachers had taken extreme approaches. Throwing me straight onto a busy highway would have overwhelmed me, likely creating trauma and resistance. Keeping me in an empty parking lot for months would have been equally ineffective, failing to stretch my capabilities. It was the careful calibration of challenge that enabled rapid progress. The same principle applies to any significant learning or growth endeavour. Whether developing leadership skills, learning a new language, or building relationships, the fastest progress comes from operating at your learning edge—where the challenge is real but not overwhelming, where mistakes are expected but not devastating, where growth is demanding but possible.

The key is recognising when we've settled into comfortable competence and deliberately seeking new challenges that push us back to that productive edge. Because while plateaus may be acceptable in some areas of life, in the domains where we truly want to excel, we must continually find ways to dance along that edge of competence where real growth occurs.

Introduce productive discomfort

When GE Healthcare set out to develop a portable electrocardiograph for rural communities, they didn't give their engineers unlimited resources and freedom. Instead, they imposed what seemed like impossible constraints: the device had to cost no more than $1 per scan, fit in a backpack, run on batteries, and be developed in just 18 months with a budget one-tenth of their usual spending. The result wasn't just successful; it was revolutionary. The constraints didn't hamper innovation; they catalysed it.

This counterintuitive relationship between constraints and performance challenges our natural instincts about creativity and

8. Embrace productive discomfort

innovation. Common wisdom suggests that to get the best results, we should remove all limitations and give teams complete freedom. Yet research by Oguz A. Acar, Murat Tarakci, and Daan van Knippenberg across 145 empirical studies showed something surprising: both individuals and organisations benefit from a healthy dose of constraints. It's only when constraints become too restrictive that they stifle creativity and innovation.

The key lies in finding what Andy Grove, former CEO of Intel, called "productive paranoia"—that sweet spot where constraints create enough tension to drive excellence without triggering paralysis. Consider three types of productive constraints:

- **Time constraints** create the urgency needed to prevent overthinking and endless refinement. Well-designed time boxes are short enough to drive focus but long enough to allow quality work, with clear milestones that create momentum and prevent procrastination.
- **Resource constraints** force teams to make deliberate choices about what truly matters rather than pursuing every possibility. Limited budgets, focused team composition, and clearly defined scope boundaries drive innovation precisely because they eliminate the paralysis that comes with unlimited options.
- **Performance constraints** establish the standards that separate acceptable from exceptional work. Challenging but achievable targets, specific quality thresholds, and measurable success criteria give teams a clear target to aim for while creating the productive tension that drives excellence.

Google famously applies this balanced approach with their "creativity loves constraints" principle. While giving employees freedom to pursue innovation through initiatives, like "20% time", they simultaneously impose strict constraints on product performance—like demanding their applications work seamlessly across all devices and load times never exceed certain thresholds. These constraints don't limit creativity; they focus it. The power of constraints lies in how they force creative problem-solving, drive prioritisation, and focus and create shared challenges that unite teams.

However, like the optimal stress level we discussed earlier, constraints must be carefully calibrated. Too few constraints lead to complacency and what psychologists call "the path of least resistance", where teams default to obvious but suboptimal solutions. Too many constraints crush creativity and motivation. The art lies in finding the right balance for each specific situation. For breakthrough innovations, looser output constraints combined with tighter process constraints seem to work best, giving teams freedom to explore radical solutions while ensuring structured collaboration. For incremental improvements, tighter output constraints with clearer success criteria tend to drive better results.

Your role is crucial in framing constraints not as limitations but as creative challenges. When the same constraint can be seen either as a frustrating roadblock or an energising challenge, skilful leaders help teams embrace the latter perspective. They create what researchers call a "strong innovation climate"—where constraints are viewed as focusing mechanisms that drive teams to do their best work.

When managed effectively, constraints don't just control risk; they become catalysts for excellence, driving teams to achieve outcomes that might never have emerged in an environment of unlimited resources and complete freedom.

Find flow as a result

Have you ever been so absorbed in a project or activity that time seemed to stand still? Perhaps you experienced a state where your actions felt effortless, decisions came naturally, and distractions faded away. Maybe you found yourself working at a level beyond your normal capabilities, with ideas flowing seamlessly and challenges that normally would frustrate you being solved with unusual clarity. If this sounds familiar, you may have experienced what psychologists call a "flow state".

Flow, first identified by psychologist Mihaly Csikszentmihalyi, represents an optimal state of consciousness where we feel and perform our best. It's that rare but powerful condition where challenge and capability meet perfectly—where we're operating at the edge of our abilities but not beyond them. What's fascinating is that flow doesn't occur when things are too easy, nor when they're too hard. It emerges precisely in that sweet spot of productive tension we've been discussing.

The conditions that create flow align remarkably well with the principles we've explored about productive tension:

- **Clear goals** provide the essential framework that allows our minds to fully engage without uncertainty pulling us out of the moment. When we know exactly what we're trying to achieve, understand the boundaries within which we're working, and receive immediate feedback on our progress, our minds can release the cognitive load of questioning and focus entirely on execution.

- **Challenge–skills balance** creates the optimal tension that makes flow possible by positioning us at the edge of our capabilities without pushing beyond them. This delicate balance—where tasks stretch our abilities without overwhelming them and difficulty increases progressively as our skills grow—creates the perfect conditions for total engagement and peak performance.
- **Deep concentration** emerges naturally when the previous conditions are met, allowing us to experience complete focus without the distractions of self-consciousness or anxiety about failure. This full immersion in the task creates a self-reinforcing cycle where deeper focus leads to better performance, which further enhances our ability to concentrate.

Research shows that people in flow states are up to 500% more productive, learn new skills more rapidly, report higher levels of fulfilment, and perform at peak capability levels. But here's where it gets interesting. Flow doesn't occur in conditions of complete freedom or absence of pressure. In fact, studies show that some level of constraint or challenge is essential for achieving flow. Too little pressure and we become bored; too much and we become anxious. Flow emerges in that optimal zone of productive tension.

Have you ever been assigned an incredibly open-ended task? Perhaps you were told to "come up with something innovative" or "redesign the process however you see fit" with no parameters, deadlines, or specific requirements. Did you feel a curious paralysis settle in? Maybe you experienced endless second-guessing, difficulty getting started, or a strange sense of demotivation despite the apparent freedom you were given. Perhaps you found yourself cycling through too many options, struggling to evaluate which direction was best, or feeling adrift without clear markers of progress.

These reactions aren't signs of creative block but rather natural responses to the absence of productive tension. Without some constraints to push against, our minds often default to familiar patterns or become overwhelmed by infinite possibilities. This is why too little pressure leads to boredom or aimlessness, while too much triggers anxiety. Flow emerges precisely in that optimal zone of productive tension. By maintaining the right level of challenge and constraint in our work, we don't just drive better outcomes; we create conditions conducive to flow states. It's another example of how some discomfort isn't just necessary for growth; it's essential for peak performance.

This brings us full circle in our discussion of failure and growth. The same conditions that allow us to learn effectively from failure—clear goals, focused attention, balanced challenge—also create the possibility for flow states. By embracing productive tension rather than avoiding it, we set ourselves up not just for better performance, but for more engaging and satisfying work experiences.

Finding freedom in disciplined focus

As we reach the end of this chapter, you might be wondering if I've contradicted everything I've argued throughout this book. After all, I've spent the previous chapters encouraging you to free yourself from the paralysing fear of failure, only to now suggest that some anxiety about failure is necessary for peak performance. Have I led you down a contradictory path? Not at all. What we're encountering isn't a contradiction but a paradox—one of those complexities that reveal deeper truths when embraced rather than simplified. The relationship between freedom and constraint, between acceptance and standards, between comfort and growth, has never been an either/or proposition. It's always been about finding the dynamic balance that allows you to perform at your best.

Nothing I've shared in this chapter negates the importance of psychological safety, the power of learning from failure, or the necessity of taking imperfect action. What I'm suggesting you consider is that transforming your relationship with failure doesn't mean eliminating all concern about outcomes—it means changing how you relate to that concern. The anxious achiever who lies awake Sunday night paralysed by fear of Monday's potential failures is not experiencing productive tension. They're trapped in a fear-based relationship with failure that diminishes rather than enhances their performance. Similarly, the professional who has become so comfortable with mediocre results that they no longer strive for excellence has lost the productive discomfort that drives growth.

The sweet spot, that target zone we've explored, lies between these extremes. It's where you care deeply about quality but don't attach your self-worth to perfection. It's where you maintain high standards while accepting that the path to meeting them includes necessary failures. Think of it as the difference between destructive fear and productive concern. Fear of failure narrows your thinking, triggers defensive behaviours, and drains your energy. Productive concern, by contrast, sharpens your focus, inspires creative problem-solving, and energises your efforts. One diminishes you; the other elevates your performance.

This distinction explains why some of the most innovative and successful people maintain seemingly contradictory mindsets. They combine unwavering standards with genuine humility. They pursue audacious goals while embracing the inevitability of setbacks. They demand excellence while creating environments where experimentation is encouraged. The true freedom doesn't come from eliminating all tension or concern about failure. It comes from transforming your relationship with that tension, from seeing it not as your enemy but as a potential ally in achieving your best work. When you learn to work with productive tension rather than against it, it becomes a source of energy rather than anxiety, of focus rather than fear.

This perspective is profoundly liberating because it frees you from the false choice between rigorous standards and psychological wellbeing. You don't have to choose between excellence and enjoyment, between achievement and authenticity. The path to your best work—and your most fulfilling experience of that work—lies in embracing the creative tension between these apparent opposites.

I encourage you to notice the quality of tension in your own work and life. Is it the destructive tension of fear and perfectionism, or the productive tension that drives growth and excellence? Are you using standards as a weapon against yourself, or as a compass to guide your development? Are you avoiding all discomfort, or learning to distinguish between the discomfort that signals danger and the discomfort that leads to growth?

Key takeaways

- Calibrate your productive tension by deliberately setting constraints on time, resources, or performance that are challenging enough to drive excellence without triggering paralysis or avoidance behaviours.
- Distinguish between exploration and execution phases in your work, applying appropriate standards to each—looser constraints when generating ideas and tighter requirements when delivering final results.
- Seek out your personal learning edge by identifying tasks that feel slightly uncomfortable yet achievable, as this zone of productive discomfort is where the fastest growth and most meaningful progress occurs.
- Frame constraints not as limitations but as creative catalysts that drive focus, prioritisation, and innovative problem-solving, particularly when communicating with teams about challenging conditions.
- Create conditions for flow states by establishing clear goals, balancing challenges with skills, and eliminating distractions—recognising that some productive tension is essential for achieving your peak performance and satisfaction.

Bringing it all together

I want to equip you with something simple yet powerful—the essence of this book distilled into a form you can share with a colleague over coffee or explain to a curious friend at a cocktail party. My hope is that as many people as possible can benefit from changing their relationship with failure, whether they've read this book or not. So, here's what to say when someone asks: "What's that book about changing your relationship with failure?"

There are four fundamental changes we need to make to gain the failure advantage:

First, break free from fear

Most of us don't realise how deeply fear of failure influences our decisions and behaviours. This fear hijacks our biology—triggering fight, flight, or freeze responses in situations where curiosity would serve us better. Even more insidiously, we tell ourselves stories about failure, like "I failed, so I am a failure" or "Failure is final", that trap us in limiting patterns.

The first step in changing your relationship with failure is simply becoming aware of these fears and stories and noticing when you're avoiding challenges because you might fail. Catch yourself when you start spinning negative narratives about what a setback means about you. This awareness itself begins to loosen failure's grip on your decisions.

Second, turn setbacks into stepping stones

Once you're aware of how fear shapes your approach to failure, you can actively reframe failure as feedback, valuable data rather than final judgement.

The key is focusing on what you can control rather than outcomes that are influenced by countless external factors. By redirecting your attention to your process, your effort, and your responses, you not only reduce anxiety but paradoxically increase your chances of achieving the results you want.

Third, choose progress over perfection

Most of us get stuck in endless preparation, waiting until we feel completely ready before taking action. The failure advantage comes when you start before you're ready, embracing imperfect action over perfect inaction. Real learning comes not from theorising but from engaging with reality, adjusting based on results, and continuing to move forward.

This shift includes embracing small wins over dramatic transformations. Significant achievements rarely come through occasional heroic efforts but through consistent, incremental progress. When you focus on systems for generating small improvements rather than fixating on dramatic outcomes, you not only reduce fear of failure but create unstoppable momentum toward your goals.

Fourth, balance safety and challenge

Your environment profoundly influences your relationship with failure, so actively shape cultures that balance psychological safety with productive challenge. Whether you lead a large organisation or simply influence your immediate circle, cultivate vulnerability to build trust while maintaining enough productive tension to drive excellence.

That's the failure advantage in a nutshell: break free from fear, turn setbacks into stepping stones, choose progress over perfection, and balance safety with challenge. These four changes won't eliminate failure from your life—they'll do something much more valuable. They'll transform failure from something to fear into a powerful catalyst for growth, innovation, and fulfilment.

Final thoughts

Writing this book has been its own lesson in embracing failure. The irony isn't lost on me that even while exploring these ideas about failure, perfectionism, and growth mindset, I've caught myself falling into old patterns—agonising over word choice, delaying completion in pursuit of an impossible standard of perfection, worrying about how readers might judge my insights. My own fixed mindset tendencies and perfectionist habits haven't magically disappeared. They still show up, still whisper their familiar doubts.

But that's precisely why I felt compelled to share these ideas. My journey with failure—from that crushing moment in the managing partner's office, through years of unconsciously limiting myself through fear, to gradually discovering a different way of relating to failure—isn't a neat story of total transformation. It's an ongoing process, a daily practice of choosing growth over protection, of catching myself when I slip into old patterns, and gently steering back toward a more productive path.

Many of you may recognise this struggle. Perhaps you too are an anxious achiever, outwardly successful but internally battling perfectionist tendencies that drain the joy from your achievements. Maybe you lie awake on Sunday nights, mind racing with all the ways things could go wrong in the week ahead. Or perhaps you've hit a plateau in your career or business, sensing that fear of failure is keeping you from taking the bold steps needed to reach the next level.

Throughout this book, we've explored a fundamentally different way of relating to failure—one that I'm still learning to embrace myself. We've seen how reframing failure as feedback can accelerate our growth and learning. We've discovered how action beats perfection (a lesson I had to keep reminding myself of while writing this very book), and how letting go of outcome obsession can paradoxically lead to better results. We've learnt the power of small steps, the importance of experimentation, and how to build environments where failure becomes not something to fear, but something to learn from.

But knowing these principles isn't enough, I know this firsthand. The real transformation comes from putting them into practice, even imperfectly. It comes from making different choices in those crucial moments when fear whispers: "Better play it safe," or perfectionism urges: "Not good enough yet." It comes from building new habits that support growth rather than protect ego, from creating systems that turn failure into learning, and from gradually developing the courage to operate at your learning edge where real progress happens.

My hope is that this book serves not just as a source of insight, but as a companion on your journey of transforming your relationship with failure. That the next time you face a challenging decision or potential failure, you'll have new tools and perspectives to draw upon. That you'll be able to replace paralysing fear with productive tension, perfectionistic paralysis with imperfect action, and outcome obsession with process mastery—even if, like me, you have to keep working at it every day. The journey won't always be smooth. You'll still experience failures. In fact, if you're applying these principles correctly, you might fail more often as you push your boundaries and take smart risks. You'll still feel the pull of fixed mindset thinking and perfectionist tendencies. But you'll have new ways to work with these challenges, to turn them from obstacles into opportunities for growth.

Most importantly, you'll discover what I'm continuing to learn myself: that the greatest gift of transforming your relationship with failure is the freedom to be fully yourself, to pursue meaningful goals without paralysis, and to find joy in the journey rather than anxiety about the destination. This isn't just about achieving more (though you likely will). It's about achieving differently—with more satisfaction, more authenticity, and more impact.

As you close this book and return to your work and life, remember that every moment presents a choice in how we relate to failure. Choose growth over protection. Choose action over perfection. Choose learning over fear. In doing so, you won't just change your relationship with failure; you'll unlock your true potential for success and satisfaction in all domains of life.

Further resources

In the process of writing this book, and on my own journey with failure, I've read and experimented with lots of ideas—the full list would be overwhelming. So, to save you the time and provide some focus, here are the top 20 resources I'd recommend exploring further. This curated collection brings together powerful books, practical frameworks, and hands-on tools I've found helpful in daily life.

Books

These works provide deeper exploration of key concepts related to failure, growth mindset, and resilience. They offer both theoretical foundations and practical applications to support your journey.

1. *Mindset: The New Psychology of Success* by Carol Dweck
   The foundational work on growth mindset psychology, presenting research that shows how our beliefs about our abilities dramatically impact our success. Dweck draws on decades of research to show how praise, criticism, and failure affect our ability to learn and grow. Her work reveals that intelligence and talent are just starting points, and it's our approach to challenges that ultimately shapes our success. In addition to the overall concept, this taught me specific techniques to shift from a fixed mindset (where failure is final) to a growth mindset (where failure is feed-

back). Particularly useful for overcoming the "I failed so I am a failure" story.

2. *Atomic Habits* by James Clear
A practical guide to building good habits and breaking bad ones through tiny, consistent changes. Clear explains how small improvements compound over time and provides a detailed framework for designing your environment to make good habits inevitable and bad habits impossible. This book provided concrete systems for turning intentions into actions through habit stacking and environment design. Perfect for implementing the "small steps to greatness" approach and creating systems that ensure consistent progress despite occasional setbacks.

3. *The Gifts of Imperfection* by Brené Brown
An exploration of courage, compassion, and connection as pathways to living wholeheartedly despite our imperfections. Brown shares insights from her research on shame and vulnerability, providing 10 guideposts for cultivating authenticity and resilience.
I thought this was a bit fluffy at first, but it helped me explore how to overcome shame-based responses to failure through practices of self-compassion and vulnerability. Particularly helpful for those struggling with perfectionism.

4. *Thinking in Bets* by Annie Duke
A former professional poker player's guide to making decisions when you don't have all the facts. Duke draws on her experience at the poker table to show how embracing uncertainty leads to better decision-making in business and life. She provides mental models for separating luck from

Further resources

skill and managing the emotional aspects of decision-making.

I never realised how all my decisions were unconscious until I read this book. It teaches how to distinguish between bad decisions and bad outcomes, helping readers understand that good processes can sometimes lead to failures due to probability and chance. Supports shifting from outcome obsession to process excellence.

5. *The Lean Startup* by Eric Ries

   A methodology for developing businesses and products through validated learning cycles. Ries combines lean manufacturing principles with agile development practices to create an approach for rapidly testing business hypotheses with minimal resources. The book includes case studies from companies of all sizes implementing these principles. As well as being a fascinating read, this Introduced me to the build-measure-learn feedback loop and the concept of "minimum viable products" that turn failure into a structured learning process. Excellent for implementing the experimentation approach to failure.

6. *Man's Search for Meaning* by Viktor Frankl

   Part memoir of surviving Nazi concentration camps and part introduction to logotherapy, it is Frankl's approach to finding meaning in all aspects of life. Through his personal story of extreme suffering, Frankl demonstrates how maintaining purpose and meaning can sustain the human spirit under the most challenging circumstances. The second part of the book outlines his therapeutic approach based on these insights.

If you ever need to "get over yourself", this is the book to read. It really shows how we live in our minds and provides profound insights into how we can choose our response to any circumstance and find meaning even in suffering. Helps reframe the stories we tell ourselves about failure.

7. *Principles* by Ray Dalio
   The billionaire investor shares his approach to life and work through a set of principles developed over decades. Dalio provides both his life principles for personal growth and work principles for building effective organisations. The book includes detailed frameworks for decision-making, feedback, and learning from mistakes that Dalio developed while building Bridgewater Associates.
   I liked the systematic approach to decision-making and learning from mistakes that has been proven in one of the world's most successful investment firms. Includes specific tools for "thoughtful disagreement" and radical transparency around failure.

8. *Conscious Business* by Fred Kofman
   A guide to building value through values, emphasising integrity, responsibility, and authentic communication in business. Kofman combines philosophical insights with practical business applications to show how consciousness transforms organisations. The book provides frameworks for having difficult conversations, making ethical decisions, and finding meaning through work.
   I've come back to this book so many times as it manages to draw out some dynamics we experience every day but may not notice. It introduces the concept of "unconditional

Further resources

responsibility" that helps readers move from blame to ownership when things go wrong. Provides frameworks for having difficult conversations about failures without blame or defensiveness.

Frameworks and models

These structured approaches provide systematic methods for implementing failure-positive practices in your work and life. They are tools I come back to often when working with individuals or teams.

1. After Action Review (AAR)
   A structured debrief process developed by the U.S. Army that uses four key questions. What was expected? What happened? Why did it happen? What can we learn? The process is designed to be brief, focused, and actionable, typically taking 30–60 minutes immediately following an event or milestone. AARs have been adapted for business use by organisations ranging from hospitals to tech companies. This turns failures from embarrassments into learning opportunities through a standardised, blame-free process and creates psychological safety while ensuring accountability. Where to find: Detailed guides are available from the U.S. Army's Center for Army Lessons Learned, and adaptations for business contexts can be found in management literature from Harvard Business Review and other business publications. The concept is also the subject of a great series for business leaders from Wharton called "Nano Tools" that you can learn and start using in 15 minutes: https://

executiveeducation.wharton.upenn.edu/wp-content/uploads/2021/06/NanoTool-2021-07.pdf

2. Ladder of Inference
   Developed by organisational psychologist Chris Argyris, this framework reveals how we move from observable data to conclusions and actions, often without awareness. The "ladder" illustrates our thinking process: we select data from what we observe, add meaning based on cultural and personal interpretations, make assumptions based on those meanings, draw conclusions, adopt beliefs, and take actions. This visual model shows how quick jumps up the ladder often lead to faulty conclusions about failures and missed learning opportunities.
   Using this framework will help you and your and teams recognise when you're making unsupported leaps from facts to interpretations, especially in failure situations. By "walking down the ladder", you can identify where thinking went wrong and separate objective evidence from subjective storytelling about failures.
   Where to find: Described in Peter Senge's *The Fifth Discipline* and good guidance at: https://thesystemsthinker.com/the-ladder-of-inference/

3. OODA loop (observe, orient, decide, act)
   A decision-making framework developed by military strategist John Boyd that emphasises rapid cycles of learning and adaptation. The model focuses on speed and agility in uncertain environments, helping decision-makers process information, recognise patterns, and take action more quickly than competitors. Originally developed for fighter

pilot combat, it has been widely adapted for business strategy and personal effectiveness.

The key takeaway here is to encourage quick iteration and learning from failure rather than extensive planning. Particularly useful in fast-changing environments where perfect information is impossible.

Where to find: There are so many resources on OODA from theory to practice, including some great 10–15-minute YouTube courses that will help you get up to speed. One summary I use is from TechTarget: https://www.techtarget.com/searchcio/definition/OODA-loop

4. The Five Whys technique

A root cause analysis method developed at Toyota that involves repeatedly asking "why?" to dig beneath surface-level explanations. The technique starts with a specific problem statement and drills down through successive layers of causation to identify underlying systemic issues. The process typically involves small groups working together to ensure different perspectives are considered. Once you do this a few times you'll find yourself drawing on the technique over and over again as it prevents superficial analysis of failures by pushing beyond immediate causes to identify systemic issues and shifts focus from blame to understanding.

Where to find: Detailed in books on lean manufacturing and quality management, and through numerous websites but one useful guide including videos can be found here: https://www.lean.org/lexicon-terms/5-whys/

5. OKR framework (objectives and key results)
   A goal-setting methodology pioneered by Intel and popularised by Google that connects measurable results to ambitious objectives. OKRs consist of an ambitious, qualitative objective that defines where you want to go, paired with three to five key results that are specific, measurable outcomes showing whether you're making progress. The framework emphasises transparency, alignment, and commitment to stretch goals, an approach that inherently acknowledges both that there is not a fixed path toward the goal and that the goal is so ambitious as not to be a certainty. It also highlights the importance of recognising progress and the need for regular retrospectives to focus on feedback and learning.
   Where to find: Made famous by Google and their overview is one of the best: https://rework.withgoogle.com/en/guides/set-goals-with-okrs#introduction

6. Design thinking
   A human-centred approach to innovation that draws from the designer's toolkit to integrate human needs, technological possibilities, and business requirements. The process typically includes five phases: empathise, define, ideate, prototype, and test. Design thinking emphasises deep user understanding, rapid prototyping, and iterative improvement based on feedback.
   Even if you don't design products or processes for a living, I think this is one of the most powerful frameworks for anyone in business because it puts the customer at the heart of everything and it embeds failure as a natural part of the creative process through prototyping and testing. The emphasis on empathy, ideation, and iteration makes failure

a valuable part of discovering solutions rather than something to avoid.
Where to find: Great resources can be found at interaction-design.org and numerous books, including *Change by Design* by Tim Brown.

Tools and Practices

These practical techniques can be implemented immediately to change how you approach failure in daily work and life. They provide concrete methods for turning principles into action.

1. Decision Journals
   A structured record of key decisions, including context, expected outcomes, and uncertainties. Decision journals capture your thinking at the time of making important choices, documenting assumptions, anticipated risks, and the reasoning behind your conclusion. Regular review of past entries creates a feedback loop for improving decision quality over time.
   I find keeping a record of decisions creates an honest feedback loop by capturing your thinking at the time of a decision, and is especially powerful to review in hindsight; both to realise what you didn't know at the time but to also recognise that you may have made the best decision given the information you had. Also powerful to recognise patterns of error or success.
   Where to find: Templates are available through Farnam Street's blog (fs.blog) and various decision-making resources. Can be adapted using any notebook or digital tool.

2. Premortem Exercises
   A team exercise where members imagine a project has failed and work backward to determine potential causes. Unlike risk assessment that asks what might go wrong, a premortem assumes failure has already occurred and asks why. This psychological shift helps overcome optimism bias and makes it safer to identify potential problems before they occur.
   This process helps teams identify potential failure points before they occur and reduces the stigma of raising concerns. It also makes failure discussion a normal part of planning rather than a post-failure autopsy.
   Where to find: Described in Gary Klein's work, including his book *Sources of Power*, and in various business management resources.

3. Personal retrospectives
   An adaptation of the agile software development practice of team retrospectives for individual growth and learning. Personal retrospectives involve setting aside time (weekly, monthly, or quarterly) to reflect on what went well, what didn't, and what adjustments to make going forward. They combine reflection, analysis, and planning in a structured format.
   This provides a structured time to reflect on what went well, what didn't, and what could be improved and creates a regular habit of learning from both successes and failures.
   Where to find: Personal retrospective formats can be found with a Google image search or there is some great guidance at: https://miro.com/miroverse/personal-retrospective-template/

Further resources

4. Uncertainty mapping (also known as the Rumsfeld matrix)
   A visual tool for mapping known knowns, known unknowns, and unknown unknowns in a project or decision. Uncertainty maps help teams explicitly identify different types of uncertainty and develop appropriate strategies for each. The process involves categorising aspects of a project or decision based on the team's current knowledge and confidence levels.
   This helps teams acknowledge and prepare for potential failure points and reduces surprise and blame when failures occur in areas of recognised uncertainty.
   Where to find: Can be created with standard visual mapping software or even simple drawing tools and good guidance at: https://www.theuncertaintyproject.org/tools/rumsfeld-matrix

5. Psychological safety assessments
   Tools for measuring and improving the level of psychological safety in teams, based on Amy Edmondson's research. These assessments typically involve surveys that measure team members' comfort with interpersonal risk-taking, such as admitting mistakes, asking questions, or challenging ideas. Results help leaders identify specific areas for improvement in team culture.
   Conducting an assessment will help you get a real picture of how your team or organisation are experiencing mistakes and failures so that you can take concrete steps for building environments where failure can be acknowledged without fear.
   Where to find: Read Edmondson's book *The Fearless Organisation* or there is good guidance at: www.leaderfactor.com/

learn/how-to-measure-psychological-safety complete with free and paid resources.

6. Learning circles
   A structured approach to group learning where team members regularly share lessons from recent failures and successes. Learning circles typically involve six to ten participants meeting on a regular schedule with rotating facilitation and clear norms for productive discussion. The format emphasises personal storytelling, collaborative problem-solving, and actionable takeaways.
   Practising this can create a routine practice for discussing failures in a supportive environment to normalise failure as part of the learning process and help extract maximum value from setbacks.
   Where to find: The Atlassian team playbook has great guidance on how to conduct the exercise with your group: https://www.atlassian.com/team-playbook/plays/learning-circle